"Here is a book that should be required reading for every seminarian and should be a gift to every pastor and church board. Thank God that Carol Howard and James Fenimore have said out loud the things that are usually expressed only through sighs and tears. The diagnosis is sound, and the prescriptions are wise indeed."
—Brian D. McLaren, author of *Do I Stay Christian?*

"Every pastor I know right now is experiencing some degree of burnout, pain, or desperation. None of us are okay. I can't think of a more important book for clergy and those who wish to help them. Howard and Fenimore speak with authority, care, grace, and knowledge. A must-read."
—Traci Smith, author of the Faithful Families series

"I wish this resource had been available when I suffered through my own brutal pastorate, leaving me burned-out and wounded to my core. It's a compassionate, life-giving, and practical guide for wounded clergy (and who among us isn't in some way?) and the people who love them."
—Martin Thielen, author of *What's the Least I Can Believe and Still Be a Christian?* and *The Answer to Bad Religion Is Not No Religion*

"Howard and Fenimore love the church and intimately know its capacity to wound its pastors. Their book is a gift to clergy and to the congregations they serve. Pastors, let them come alongside you and accompany you with care through the wounds of ministry and into greater healing and wholeness."
—Cody J. Sanders, Associate Professor of Congregational and Community Care Leadership, Luther Seminary

"With every turn of the page, pastors will see themselves reflected in the stories of congregational leaders facing the fragility and flaws of Christian communities. As in holding up a mirror to ourselves, the text will return images of wounds that crave for healing. Whether these wounds show up as skin-level scratches or deep cuts on the soul, Howard and Fenimore's book offers us a much-needed balm."
—José R. Irizarry, President, Austin Presbyterian Theological Seminary

"Healthy churches need healthy pastors, which means every pastor needs this book. *Wounded Pastors* charts the course for clergy to live out their vocation without sacrificing their health, privacy, and jobs in the process. Howard and Fenimore help clergy feel seen and heard as they offer tangible first steps for weary and wounded clergy, whether on the job or recovering from it."

—Carol Harston, pastor and founder, Eden Hill Initiative

"In *Wounded Pastors*, Howard and Fenimore offer us a compassionate resource for clergy to pragmatically care for themselves. When we think of care as something more than a fuzzy feeling proximate to love or kindness or even ministry but as a necessity for survival, something like food or air, then we see just how important this book is for sustaining our vocation. The authors come alongside us to help us recognize and engage actively in the ongoing healing of our wounds so that we might see how we courageously enact healing in our churches."

—Mihee Kim-Kort, copastor of First Presbyterian Church, Annapolis, Maryland, and author of *Outside the Lines: How Embracing Queerness Will Transform Your Faith*

Wounded Pastors

Wounded Pastors

*Navigating Burnout, Finding Healing,
and Discerning the Future of Your Ministry*

CAROL HOWARD

AND

JAMES FENIMORE

WESTMINSTER
JOHN KNOX PRESS
LOUISVILLE • KENTUCKY

First edition
Published by Westminster John Knox Press
Louisville, Kentucky

24 25 26 27 28 29 30 31 32 33—10 9 8 7 6 5 4 3 2 1

Book design by Sharon Adams
Cover design by Luisa Dias

Library of Congress Cataloging-in-Publication Data is on file
at the Library of Congress, Washington, DC.

ISBN-13: 978-0-664-26845-9

Most Westminster John Knox Press books are available at special quantity discounts when purchased in bulk by corporations, organizations, and special-interest groups. For more information, please e-mail SpecialSales@wjkbooks.com.

To our fellow wounded pastors

Contents

Part Three: Nurturing Our Growth

Acknowledgments

We want to thank those who looked at early drafts, carefully edited them, and gave vital feedback, especially Claire Brown, Ruth Everhart, Robin Lostetter, Katherine Pater, and Derrick Weston. Along the way, we have spoken to many wounded pastors—some we can name and some we cannot. We wanted to make sure that we listened to people who had practical experience beyond the studies and our personal experience. We have especially sought counsel from those who have been hurt and who have navigated the pain with incredible grace. They helped us with best practices and exercises. Though we can't acknowledge everyone, here are a few people who helped form the content. Melissa Lynn Allison, Susan Arsee, Leslieanne Adkins Braunstein, Patricia Calahan, Meghan Davis-Brass, Jennifer DiFrancesco, Michelle Favreault, Kathy Genus, Doug Hagler, David Hansen, Daniel Haugh, Ogun Holder, Tad Hopp, Emma Horn, Erin Kobs, Heather McCance, Mary Louise McCullough, Lara Blackwood Pickrel, Paul Schneider, Brooklynn Smith, Scott Spence, Dave Stradling, Michael Terrell, Mindi Welton-Mitchell, Courtney Steininger, and Shannon Weston made up a wise focus group. Ryan Larkin spent many hours giving critical insight and talking through the contents of the book.

We want to thank Jessica Miller Kelley for her support, counsel, and editing, and for the wonderful team at Westminster John Knox Press for ushering this book to all of you.

I (Carol) want to thank my daughter, Calla, for her beautiful inspiration through it all.

I (James) want to thank my wife, Alison, and children Kayla, David, Ashley, Olive, and Eliot for their support and encouragement.

Introduction

When I (Carol) wrote a previous book titled *Healing Spiritual Wounds*, I focused on helping people who had been wounded by the church. I hoped that people who had been raised to understand that Christianity had a vengeful, anti-science God who celebrated misogyny and homophobia would be able to embrace a God who is a loving Creator, delighting in all expressions of humanity and affections. I wanted to have a resource for those who had been wounded by Christian nationalism, religiously fueled racism, or pedophile priests. I geared the book toward laypeople, including those who tried on atheism but kept feeling drawn back to God and needed a healthier view of religion to support their spiritual longings.

The book frustrated many of my clergy friends because it didn't talk about the wounds that *pastors* experience in the church. So I began a book that would address that particular perspective.

When I (James) transitioned from congregational ministry to working as a psychotherapist, I discovered a commonality in my clergy clients. Story after story included the wounds they had received while serving in their vocation. During the pandemic, and especially during lockdown, clergy suffered. I quickly learned telehealth and sat in my home office busier than ever doing essentially the same job, only now through a screen. My clergy clients didn't find this an easy transition. Clergy had always lived with unreasonable expectations, but now the demands were impossible. As clergy tried to navigate this new isolated landscape, they paid an enormous price and had the wounds to show for it.

We (Carol and James) worked together creating online services during the pandemic. As we set up teleprompters, adjusted cameras, and arranged backgrounds, we talked about what we heard and experienced. The stories of churches wounding their leaders flowed. We sensed a general longing for someone to name the challenges that ministers face, not so that we could wallow in self-pity and bitterness, but so that we could diagnose the problem and heal.

So we wrote this book on what we saw from our various roles—as pastors, as a therapist, as consultants, as lecturers, and as friends. James talked about systems theory that helped explain the experiences we shared. We listened to people and collected stories. We tried to get a variety of perspectives from pastors in different racial-ethnic groups, with different gender identities, abilities, and sexual orientations, although we confess that there are inevitably blind spots in our observations.

This book is for and about healthy pastors. Unfortunately, narcissistic or sociopathic pastors exist and cause great damage to congregations and their members. Carol addressed the damage that those pastors can do in her previous work. However, in this book, we want to talk to pastors who don't have a major personality disorder, even though they might struggle with anxiety, addiction, or depression.

We also assume that the pastors reading this book will have a basic, healthy theology. We believe that God loves us. There are no barriers to that love; no gender identity, sexual orientation, race, ethnicity, or disability can keep us from the love of God. God does not discriminate.

As we interviewed people for this book, some asked if we would address the churches that wound pastors, if we would write to the pastor's family, and if we would talk about what other church professionals (music directors, Christian educators, youth directors, etc.) endure. Of course, all church leaders are welcome to read the book and pass it along. Professors who have never served a parish and members who only know church from the perspective of the pews could have a lot to learn. But at some point we must acknowledge that every subject matter creates a chain reaction of curiosity and that no book can be exhaustive. This subject is no exception. So we write to pastors while we hope that this book can give insight to others also.

We include reflection questions and prompts in each short chapter that you might use with a clergy group or at a retreat, or journal through individually. Feel free to pick and choose between the exercises or to skip them altogether.

This is an incredibly important time to be a pastor. The world needs the tools and gifts that healthy ministers can bring. To that end, we cannot ignore what pains us. We must speak to the hurt and find healing.

Part One

Identifying Our Pain

Chapter One

Starting Our Journey

The COVID-19 pandemic was raging when I (Carol) signed up for a clergy trip to Israel and Palestine. The newspaper's daily CDC maps mutated from a dangerous red to an appalling purple as the Omicron variant proved its dominance and took hold of the world's hospitals. I imagined being trapped in a metal tube, flying with hundreds of people and no social distance. Then, while holding my breath, I paid a deposit, purchased airline tickets, and bought trip insurance.

I was just *that* desperate for a break.

I had started a new position during the pandemic. I dropped straight into difficult discussions about sanctuary gatherings, mask mandates, and vaccine requirements. The social settings where ecclesial bonding would ordinarily take place no longer existed. So I navigated a myriad of tricky situations with no social capital to spend. With that came the stressors of moving across the country, selling a home, and transitioning back into a settled pastorate. I also had the personal heartaches of a family death and a newly empty nest.

The congregation didn't know me. We tried to bond as members called and left lasagna on the porch. As the pastoral honeymoon quickly dissolved into a harsh reality, the pandemic kept us distanced. There were no lunch appointments, dinner parties, or choir.

I had few professional friends in the area. COVID put a halt to the denominational meetings and clergy gatherings that had given me life during my ministry. Instead, I greeted my new colleagues through postage-stamp boxes on Zoom. We stared out of our flat screens with our dead eyes, with no chance for small talk during breaks.

Conferences had been canceled. In previous years I had traveled and, while keynoting, had been able to connect with pastors, authors, and editors. But those engagements vanished as the virus surged.

Social media, which had provided a wonderful source of community for fifteen years, had become dangerous. After a group of clergy coordinated an intense Twitter attack that raged far too long and ended with a rape threat and a police report, I had to step away. That meant I cut myself off from the constant comforting chatter that had allowed me to maintain loose social connections with people around the world.

I felt isolated. I was a clay vessel—dry and brittle, chipped in places, and utterly empty inside.

That's why even a global pandemic couldn't keep me from attempting some sort of spiritual renewal. Plus, I knew that Abbie Huff and Ryan Larkin, a couple of pastors who always made me laugh, had not yet backed out. With them around, it would be a good trip. In Tel Aviv, I met another minister, Penny Hogan, who traveled with us. Within a few hours, I realized that pandemic pastoring had worn out other clergy as well.

We had a short worship service every day. Our leader, Rev. Anne Weirich, designed the liturgy, readings, and meditations so we could move through the settings on a deeper level. Aware of our fragile states, Anne never forced the pastors to become the designated liturgists. She allowed the clergy to lead but took care not to put us in charge when we didn't have the spiritual stamina.

We traveled to Magdala, home of Mary Magdalene, the woman who washed the feet of Jesus with her tears, anointed them with her perfume, and dried them with her hair. One of the twelve disciples became annoyed by the extravagant gesture, but Jesus explained that Mary was preparing him for his death. He said that whenever we told the good news, we were to do it in her memory. The gospel should always include the story of Mary, who took care of her teacher, who somehow knew that friends would betray and deny him. Mary poured out her tears, and that gave Jesus the strength to face his devastation.

Of course, the acknowledgment didn't happen the way Jesus instructed. The Gospel writers didn't remember Mary well. Her bio is sketchy at best, and her name is completely left out of one account. Our traditions offer conflicting narratives, as if we can't figure out if Mary was a demon-possessed sex worker or a woman from a loving and stable home who became Jesus' top student (the one who sat at his feet), or all of the above. Now we must make do with this fuzzy amalgamation of various women with no clear identity.[1]

Understanding the two years that the clergy had gone through, Anne remembered Mary. She took us to a church by the Sea of Galilee that had been built in Mary's honor. We gathered in a room that had a giant mural of Jesus' feet. Echoing Mary's care, Anne asked the group of pilgrims to surround Abbie, Penny, Ryan, and me. They laid hands on us and prayed for us. She anointed us with oil. We felt a little guilty, like the gesture was too extravagant. We knew the people surrounding us also needed prayers; they were all church leaders, mission directors, and college administrators. But we received the gifts.

With our heads bowed in the center of extended arms, muttered blessings, and flowing tears, I broke. Every dry and brittle piece of me crumbled and turned to dust. I started crying. It was a big, ugly sort of release. I couldn't get ahold of enough tissues to maintain any composure, so I just gave up.

After I loosened that rusty tap of tears, it kept flowing. The next day I stood in a garden, and water began streaming down my face. I walked into a church, and it happened again. I began to cry at lakes and rainbows, at ancient walls and new barriers. I began to feel the sorrow of that holy and fraught land, where blood had spilled and seemed to scream out from the ground. The heavy sadness of so many pilgrims pressed down on me.

I don't cry often, so each time it happened I felt bewildered, looking down at another wet tissue and saying, "I—I don't know where all of this is coming from."

"Your tears are precious," Anne told me. "God is storing them, keeping them in a bottle," she said, echoing Psalm 56:8.

I am used to containing experiences with words, organizing them, and making sense of them through the complicated rules of syntax and grammar. But this was something different. The events from the past year had traveled from my brain to that emotional pool in my gut, and it needed release. With friends around, I had enough security and support that I could finally let go. With the tears, the dust was restored to clay.

Through the next year, as I built relationships with members of the congregation, I ventured to heal and decided to keep working as a pastor. The experience led me to wonder, *How have pastors handled this collective trauma? What do we do when we've been wounded by the church? How do we recognize the pain? How do we rebuild and find wholeness? How do we grow after the experience?*

As I asked these questions out loud, I found other ministers dealing with the same issues. With the pandemic exacerbating normal church tensions, making them feel insurmountable, many began to leave the pastorate. When I spoke with the fleeing clergy confidentially, they cited toxic work environments as the reason.

As I mulled over concerns with my friend and colleague James, we each mentioned that we were writing books on the subject. So we decided to write a book together. We are both pastors, and James has additional experience and expertise as a judicatory leader and psychotherapist. We figured that our different experiences might help clergy who are traveling this path toward healing, because while I decided to stay in the pastorate, James made the decision to leave.

My phone rang at 6 a.m. When I (James) reached for the receiver, the caller ID information fully roused me.

"Good morning, Bishop," I said.

"Yes, James. I just learned some disturbing news. I heard from one of your colleagues that you are getting a divorce. I must say, I'm very disappointed that you didn't share this with me."

"Bishop, I . . ."

"No, no, no. I want you and your wife to be in my office on Wednesday morning at 10 a.m."

"Bishop, I'm not sure she'll agree to come."

"You make sure she's there." And with that, he hung up.

I looked around the room in dazed confusion.

It wasn't the first time our marriage was on the brink. Before I had been appointed a district superintendent (a mid-judicatory leader in the United Methodist Church), we found ourselves in crisis. At the time, I had blamed myself. I had worked as the senior pastor of a downtown church and studied as a Ph.D. candidate. I had been so busy that I held myself responsible for neglecting my wife. I had thought, *Why didn't I see this happening?*

We had worked hard to salvage the marriage. We had both agreed that we wanted to stay in the relationship and recommitted ourselves to each other. We hadn't shared our struggles with anyone, just wanting to put them in the past, and that's what I thought we had done. I wasn't trained in psychotherapy at the time; still, I had known intuitively that keeping things secret and burying our deep wounds was probably not the best approach. But that's what we decided.

I worked as a district superintendent for a few years, then planned to return to pastoral ministry. I was appointed to a wonderful progressive congregation and looked forward to the transition. A few weeks before I started the new church, I discovered my wife wanted out. We again talked about what we could to do to salvage the marriage, but it didn't work. She planned to divorce me and soon had the papers served. I walked around in shock, trying to figure out what to do next. This time I reached out to friends, family, and colleagues. The next day I received the call from my bishop.

I assumed the bishop would be offering counsel to help us stay together, so I was surprised that my wife was willing to go with me to his office. After driving two hours in silence, we arrived. My new district superintendent greeted us and explained that he would be present for the meeting.

I suddenly realized that my bishop had not orchestrated a pastoral care moment. He called us here to find out what I did to mess up my marriage so he could bring charges against me.

The bishop asked me why I was divorcing my wife. I glanced at her. She looked at me, then looked at the floor. Then with evident pain and embarrassment, my wife explained that I didn't want to end the marriage—that it was her decision. The bishop paused, process-ing this information. The awkward and painful silence that followed was probably only a few seconds long, but it felt endless. He closed the meeting with a prayer and abruptly sent us off.

At my weakest and darkest moment, the institutional church gave me no comfort but instead inflicted more pain and devastating wounds.

A few days later, a colleague told me that the bishop was reconsid-ering my appointment to the nice progressive church. He reasoned that they had accepted a married pastor, not a soon-to-be-divorced pastor. When asked, that wonderful congregation affirmed that they would accept me and then reached out to see how I was doing.

I spent three years at that amazing church. After being deeply wounded, I found healing there. The congregation gave me hope that ministry could still happen within a church. They had some of the usual church problems, but they also loved and cared for one another.

During my time of healing, I realized that I couldn't go through that sort of heartache again. I needed to transition to a role that would allow me to still be part of the church without being dependent on it. So I made the difficult and painful decision to leave congregational ministry as a pastor.

Although one of us has an experience of staying and the other has an experience of leaving the pastorate, we both worked to heal and find abundance. And we realized that part of that process included making meaning out of what had happened. We wanted to trace the steps we had taken. We read books, articles, and journals on family systems, trauma, resilience, forgiveness, and meaning, looking inside and outside of the church for research and support. And we listened to hundreds of clergypersons who were figuring out their own path. We realized that so many of our situations were similar. We experi-enced many of the same fears, contexts, and characters.

A pastor's wounds can be extraordinarily painful because they col-lect a particular emotional toll. For many of us, we became pastors because church was a literal sanctuary for us. We found God and healing in that space. We first woke up to the Spirit surrounding us as the flames crackled at that youth group campfire, as church members lavished love and acceptance on us after a divorce, or as they helped to put us back together after a parent's death. We speak of the church as a beloved community, as the body of Christ. All of these lofty ideals come into play when church members hurt us. Their rejection feels like looking at the back side of God. We feel abandoned. In the worst cases, since God used the church to heal us, it can also feel like the church is throwing punches for the Almighty.

We offer this book to pastors who feel burned-out and wounded, even as we know that we often have the best job in the world.[2] We must acknowledge when we have a difficult time getting out of bed and putting on our clothes. We feel exhausted, working at maximum capacity, and yet we hear constant feedback that we do not do enough. The endless list of people we should have visited, things we ought to have done, and ways we need to improve looms over us. The work is never complete.

It is so difficult to be a pastor in this particular time. Anxiety levels within churches are through the roof. To minister in these anxious congregations means trying to live up to every congregant's demands of what they think a pastor ought to be and do. If that isn't bad enough, denominations place unrealistic expectations on what the role of a pastor is. United Methodist pastors are familiar with the responsibilities and duties of elders in the 2016 edition of *The Book of Discipline of the United Methodist Church*. It contains a completely unfeasible set of duties that only makes this vocation more difficult. Other denominations may offer similarly fantastical job descriptions for its clergy.[3]

Sometimes in the midst of impossible demands we need to connect with people who understand and find the balm that will heal our wounds. That is the time when we need to begin this journey.

Reflection Prompts

Buy a journal, notebook, or a composition book. You will need one for the prompts that follow each chapter.

1. *Create space.* Make a small space in your home that feels safe and comfortable. It could be inside a closet, in your bedroom—anywhere you

can feel okay taking time for yourself. Use this space for your journaling, spiritual exercises, and prayer as you work through this book. Make sure that this safe space has a comfortable place to sit with your feet flat on the ground or (if it's comfortable) to sit directly on the floor. You may want to add a candle, printed Bible verses that speak to you, or images of heroes, saints, or God that make you feel safe and loved.

2. *Reflect on the wound.* After setting aside 30 minutes of uninterrupted time, write, "Where does it hurt?" on the top of a page. Answer the question as honestly as you can. Think about the pain in your present call and your past ones. Try not to sugarcoat things or add a spiritual twist if that doesn't feel honest right now. You may not be at a place of resolution. Honor that.

3. *Scan your body.* Be aware of what is happening in your body as well as your ministry. Take a couple of minutes to breathe. Mentally scan your head, neck, chest, gut, legs, and feet. Is there a place in your body where you feel pain? Are you carrying stress in your gut, neck, or lower back? Take notice of what you feel, and write it down.

Chapter Two

Finding Our People

Jesus emerges from the wilderness starving from forty days without food and weakened from struggling with all the temptations of the universe. Meanwhile Roman soldiers march out to the banks of the Jordan River, looking for John the Baptizer. It doesn't take the men long to find him. A steady stream of people gathered to hear the prophet's fiery sermons, which included hot takes on royal relationships. The soldiers arrest John.

With his cousin locked up, Jesus understands that he is stepping into a problematic ministry context, fraught with turmoil and betrayal. So the first thing Jesus does is gather friends. He borrows a boat from Simon and asks him to hang out. Then he meets Andrew, Simon's brother, and invites him along too. Going out of his way to encounter people, he calls some of them to travel with him (the disciples) and some to host him in their homes (Mary, Martha, and Lazarus), and others he simply loves even though they decide not to follow him (the rich young ruler). People complain about Jesus and his friends: "The Son of Man has come eating and drinking, and you say, 'Look, a glutton and a drunkard, a friend of tax collectors and sinners!'" (Luke 7:34).

But that doesn't deter him. One tax collector even becomes part of his inner circle. Jesus focuses on friendships until he has his entourage. He teaches that love between friends is the greatest love that we can practice, and he makes eating and drinking with friends a sacred act.

Given our exemplar, how did pastoring become such a lonely profession?

"Nothing could have prepared me for this isolation," Jacob said as he met with Carol for breakfast at a conference. Jacob worked as an Episcopal priest in a rural southern town. He felt called to small congregations. Yet as a gay man, he felt it impossible to date or even socialize. The church functioned as Jacob's income, shelter, and call. On top of that, since his congregation was the only LGBTQ-affirming community space in the town, it had also become his sole social outlet. Every part of him became enmeshed with the congregation. So Jacob felt emotionally unprepared when a leader in his congregation began to sabotage his work. When the bully kept destroying things, the other members refused to stand up for Jacob. Instead, they worked to protect and placate the saboteur, and the members consistently requested that Jacob apologize to him and beg him to come back to church. When Jacob refused, things fell apart. Jacob didn't have anyone to call because all of his friends were in the church. He stood utterly alone.

Jacob's experience reminds us that we need to find our people. We cannot depend on church members as our only friends. This can be difficult. For many of us, our church was always our main source of friendship, and understanding the congregation differently can be challenging. Many of us became pastors because we got so much out of church—spiritually, emotionally, and socially. Ever since we can remember, our lives have revolved around youth groups, mission trips, and choir practice. We may have figured out that we needed to go to seminary when we realized that we were the last one in the sanctuary every Sunday. We turned out the lights because our lives made sense within those sacred walls. It can be startling to realize that as pastors we might need to form a particular detachment from church members and think about friendships within the congregation differently. Why is this important?

Keeping boundaries around church friendships can give us self-protection. Though we have high ideals for our congregations, they are imperfect organizations, bodies made up of difficult people. We manage a group that longs for congregational niceness and cultivates strong group-think tendencies, so bullies tend to flourish in churches. Even the most well-intentioned members can let us down when we become the church troll's latest victim, because they will often seek a veneer of peace over the pastor's well-being.

When the pastor has obvious favorites, it can cause rifts in the congregation. Creating a close group of friends from within the congregation sets up an "in crowd" that has more sway over decision-making than the official leadership. Having close friends within the church becomes even more complicated when we desperately need to talk *about* the church. Or we can't honestly open up to a church member because that might compromise another parishioner.

True friendship has a mark of mutuality. It's a give-and-take of generosity, invitations, and support. When we move into the professional realm, our role shifts, and it's no longer appropriate for members to meet our need for intimacy and affection. It's not their job. It would be like spending an hour in therapy, attempting to solve our counselor's marital problems. If we do encounter a congregation that functions to serve its pastor's emotional demands, then we often find a narcissist in the minister's role.

Church members and pastors can form an unhealthy bond if our emotional reserves dry up and we use members as the sole resource to satisfy our need for love. A congregation might do a decent job of it for a while, but churches are not designed or called to meet the socio-emotional requirements of pastors. That doesn't mean our needs go away. It does mean that we have to find other outlets to meet them. Pastors deserve friends who can provide emotional support in our crises.

We also need friendships that can last beyond a particular call. We have to end our friendships when we leave a church, and that's super hard when we have become emotionally dependent on our members.

All former pastors who maintain close friendships with previous parishioners think that they are the exception. They swear that they are not hurting the church. "I *never* talk about the congregation when I go on those weeklong camping trips with the elders!" a pastor protests. "I spend every Thanksgiving with the lay leader's family, but that has *nothing* to do with the fact that she can't stand the new pastor!" But we all know the truth. Each time a former pastor hosts prior parishioners at her annual Super Bowl celebration, she prioritizes her own emotional needs over the health of the congregation.

When a former pastor disregards the professional courtesy of maintaining distance after leaving a congregation, it damages the ability of the new pastor to form bonds. The present pastor desperately tries to establish relationships, but he feels like he's on a date with a person who can't stop talking about her ex. "He was perfect! He never did anything wrong!" The ex left three years ago, but the breakup never sticks because the ex keeps texting every time he's lonely.

Of course, even with those warnings, we do need to form friendships within the church. Friendship is often the glue that bonds our church community together. We simply must do it while understanding that there are different types of friendship.

Views of Friendship

Friendship comes in different varieties, and the ways we form and maintain relationships change, depending on our context. Cultural understandings have affected our friendships, even as classic views of friendship have stood for thousands of years. Realizing who our friends are and what role they play in our lives can become important.

Social media made the term "friend" so ubiquitous that it can be confusing. We might perceive that someone is a close friend because certain algorithms make that person show up at the top of our feed each time we check into our favorite platform. In actuality, they may barely know who we are. Also, our basic human interactions have reverted to elementary modes, as a heart button endeavors to replace an embrace and a smiley icon strains to signify emotional depth.

Many pastors who live in rural areas only have access to digital friendships, so those connections can become crucial to clergy well-being. But as we spend time on social media, we should become vigilant about making sure that those loose online friendships develop depth and resonance. If possible, we can use our online bonds to enhance in-person experiences. In person, we're able to exchange hugs and physical touches. We can smell our friends and sense their mood and well-being in ways we can't through a flat screen.

Our recent cultural understandings of gender dynamics have both constrained and freed our friendships. On one hand, researchers worry that homophobia has hindered friendship and affection between men.[1] Straight men often do not have friendships outside of their spouses.[2]

On the other hand, new understandings of friendship have flourished with the recognition of different sexual identities. "I have a gay husband," an acquaintance told Carol. She explained that she was married to her husband but that she also had a gay best friend she also described as her "husband." They had made a deep covenant to one another as friends. The term *queerplatonic* has been coined as people have endeavored to describe committed intimate relationships that are not romantic in nature.[3]

Even with everything that has changed with the internet and our understanding of sexual identities, some forms of friendship have remained since the time of the ancient philosophers. We have friends who are useful, pleasurable, or good.[4]

James and Carol both have negotiated *friendships of utility*, relationships that emerge with a practical end in mind. When James was a district superintendent in the United Methodist Church, people often sidled up to him in the hope of securing a better position. But when his job changed, so did the friendships. People who once praised him were suddenly absent.

As a writer, Carol hears from many people when they want a favor—a podcast interview, manuscript endorsement, or book promotion. Then when she is no longer useful for furthering their status, or if the minor denominational celebrity buzz around her fades, she never hears from them again.

Pastors often encounter faithful careerists who network endlessly for denominational power. We also develop friends in our congregations, knowing that we may not share deep emotional mutuality with them but that our utilitarian relationship with them is important. Because of the nature of our callings and the ways we must move about in our churches and communities, we can become so adept at utilitarian friendships that we forget there is any other kind.

However, we can also have *friendships for pleasure*. We spend time with certain people because of their spark. They're fun and make us feel good. We invite these friends to our dinner parties because they time their jokes perfectly and dish out flattery flawlessly. We fall in and out of love with them, sometimes in the same afternoon.

Then there are *true friendships*, which are based on goodness. True friends remain, even if you recently took a status hit, if you're getting slammed on social media, or if you feel consumed by a stress that mutes your ability to have fun. True friends come over with a bottle of wine when you tell them that your trusted ally gave you a vote of no confidence. They go hiking with you and spend the afternoon listening to your stories on repeat as you sort out what went wrong. When you begin to rehash a recent trauma by saying, "Stop me if I've told you this before," they never stop you. They know that you need to keep repeating it.

Not only that, but true friends call you. When they're going through a divorce or they find out their kid is having a health issue, you are on top of their "favorites" in their phone list.

As Jesus told us, there is no greater love than when one gives up one's life for a friend. And "giving up your life" doesn't just mean leaping on a grenade or being nailed to a cross. It also entails the quotidian acts of eating cold takeout, listening to repeated stories, and packing U-Haul boxes. It includes a mutuality that flows back and forth. We need someone who checks in on us after we lost our temper irrationally and notices that we stopped eating. This goodness, the love for persons in themselves, is the greatest goal of a friendship.

It is essential that we find our people, which is a challenge for most pastors. We might move a lot, so we must go through the process of initiating friendships regularly. Outside of the church, ordinary people might react to us in awkward ways when they find out what we do. They get nervous, apologizing for cursing in front of us and looking over our shoulder for someone else to save them from the conversation. Or they become too excited, and we know that we have just met Ned Flanders, and we try to back away slowly.

We might have a hard time stepping back from our role. We can become so used to being the one on whom people rely that we don't know how to manage the mutuality of friendships. As one pastor reflected, "I have a lot of friends who ask things of me, but I have very few friends I can go to when I need help."

We might not be able to take off that metaphorical clergy collar, and it makes us want to problem-solve or preach at our friends instead of sitting with them and saying, "I'm so sorry. That sounds terrible."

We also may have difficulty claiming our role. How often have you been in a social setting where someone asks what you do and you hesitate to answer? You know you are likely to hear about this person's problems with organized religion, or why this person doesn't attend church. At the very least, you know that when you identify as clergy, the conversation after that will not be the same as it would have been without that identification.

In addition to the normal awkwardness of the clergy role, our culture has experienced the disintegration of many of our in-person social institutions and groups. Church attendance is down, which reflects similar trends in garden clubs, bowling leagues, quilting groups, and service clubs.[5] During the pandemic, everyone got so used to Zoom that we rarely have in-person meetings, even as things have become safer. If we are involved in a nonprofit board or engage in denominational work, teleconferencing doesn't allow any chance of grabbing lunch, conversing over coffee, or even sharing a sideways glance. Zoom calls have taken away another one of the precious few ways that we develop friendships.

If you have a spouse, that person can often provide a great escape and balance to church life. Yet spouses may have limits to their tolerance when it comes to church drama. You might need to check in with your spouse before launching into the latest ecclesial intrigue.

Connection

True friendships are not only a good idea, but we absolutely need them. Throughout this book we will refer to Bowen Family Systems Theory. Murray Bowen, a psychiatrist, developed a model of how we relate to one another. Bowen studied the interactions of thousands of patients over decades to develop and improve the theory. One of the foundational understandings is that we are social beings who need to connect with others. Even those of us who call ourselves introverts need social connection.

For Bowen, the worst thing you can do to your family, friend group, or church is to cut them off.[6] Cutting people off is one way we might respond to the difficulties of these relationships. It is an extreme example of how to deal with problems—to not deal with them at all. We all have the embarrassing uncle or the narcissistic cousin that we wish wasn't in the family. Finding a way to keep connected to people like this and work through our differences with them is an extremely important life lesson that helps us deal with the embarrassing parishioner or the self-centered music director.

This doesn't mean that you need to be close to everyone in your family or your congregation. There are circumstances where breaking connection is required for safety reasons. In abusive relationships, any connection can cause harm. Yet in most cases, the bond can come in different forms. Sometimes you can only manage a distant relationship, but that is still connection. When you have toxic individuals with whom you need to connect, it requires you to find ways to keep distance.

For instance, Andre is the pastor of a small rural congregation. He finds it difficult to get volunteers to work on projects around the church, except for one person who is always willing to help—Joe. Joe assumes that because he works so much around the church that he has a special friendship with the pastor. Joe shows up uninvited to the parsonage early in the morning or late in the evening and asks to check on things in the house. Andre realizes his own role in creating this unhealthy relationship with Joe, and so he begins to find ways to create distance in their relationship. He stops calling Joe to help on the church projects. He doesn't endorse Joe for trustee of the church. And finally, he lets Joe know how he feels when Joe shows up unannounced at the parsonage. Through all of these actions that Andre takes, Joe is able to build a healthy distance. At the same time, Andre doesn't ignore Joe. He still speaks with him at church and even visits him at his home. He keeps connection while adding distance from the toxic behavior.

Relationships in any form (family, friends, or parishioners) that make us uncomfortable should lead us to ask questions about ourselves: *Why do I feel uncomfortable in the presence of my grandmother? Is it the way she speaks? Is it her lack of understanding of what my life is like? Is it her age and my own fears of mortality?* We can dig deep with these questions as we try to understand what causes the feelings within us. We tend to think the other persons are the problem, but they are who they are. Our lack of acceptance is part of who we are, and understanding our discomfort is an opportunity to help us grow a bond with those around us.

Our lifelong task is to open ourselves to new relationships and deepen our current bonds. Exploring ourselves and our relationships isn't a very easy thing to do. We often prefer to ignore the difficult people in our lives. Developing healthy relationships is foundational to our health as persons and as pastors.

So how do we begin? We need to recognize our relationship patterns when it comes to making friends. Bowen says that people can have a tendency to become fused or to cut off too easily when establishing new friendships. Our goal is to work for secure relationships.[7]

If a person tends to fuse with another person, it means that her identity becomes tied up with her friendships. She might feel nervous about initiating friendships because she fears rejection. But once she is over that initial hurdle, she develops intimacy quickly. She allows people to get to know all sides of her personality, taking off the masks and being vulnerable. She also tends to overshare, spilling out too much information about her life without any reciprocal exchange of confidences. She can be so generous that she depletes herself. A fused friend can feel anxious about the relationship, especially when the other person is absent. When a friend doesn't respond to a text, she fears being ghosted. She might read anger and hostility when a friend leaves a light-hearted and sarcastic comment on her social media feed. She feels comfortable providing support, but she hates asking for it because she doesn't want to be a burden.

On the other hand, a person might tend toward cutoff, or to avoid friendships. He doesn't initiate friendships. When people initiate friendships with him, he tends to play hard to get, rejecting invitations to hang out, even when he really wants to be there. The friendships he does have tend to be shallow. He doesn't communicate much about his life, especially things that make him feel weak or vulnerable. He is not generous, and he tends to be suspicious of other people's motives. When a friend is absent, he forgets about that person. He feels burdened when people ask for support, and he tends to put his own needs above those of others.

If you see yourself in one of the patterns above, then know that we can all work toward healthy, secure friendships. Healthy friends seek connection and initiate friendships, extending and receiving invitations. They enter into friendships assuming that the other persons like them. When they share confidences, they check in with their friends, asking them questions, understanding that personal disclosure is an act of mutuality. They are generous, but they have boundaries around their generosity so that they do not deplete themselves. They have learned to prioritize their own needs as well as the needs of others. When a friend is absent, they assume that the connection of love and respect remains.

How can we meet friends? We have to be intentional about it. Since we're no longer in seminary and we can't find our friends solely in church, we need to find another space where we can interact with people on a regular basis. Consistent exposure to other people allows connections to form.

When you interact regularly with other people, you might find someone who is particularly interesting or funny. You'd like to get to know that person. Then you need to initiate. You can ask for a phone number and extend an invitation to coffee or lunch. If you like hosting dinners, you can set up a potluck.

As the relationship unfolds, you watch for mutuality. As pastors, we might be used to giving so generously of ourselves and never expecting any affection or care in return. While that might be appropriate in our pastor/parishioner relations, it's not a sign of a healthy friendship. We need to make an intentional shift from utilitarian friendship to true friendship. When people share confidences with us, we can reciprocate. When we need support, we can ask. When people confide a problem to us, it will no longer be our job to give spiritual guidance, practical directives, or an impromptu sermon. Instead, we listen and nod, knowing that there might not be much that we can do. We can be generous and receive generosity in return.

As we talked with pastors in various contexts, we asked them how they made friends. They offered the following suggestions.

Find a hobby. A lot of people develop a hobby or tap into one they've had for a long time. Activities such as gaming, writing, reading, cooking, gardening, painting, hiking, creating art, or crafting are good options. A hobby might include a pet. For instance, rescuing animals, going to dog parks, training therapy pets, or bonding over unusual pets will give you the chance to connect with people. Choose or adapt a hobby so you can meet with other people regularly.

Use continuing education for connection. Maybe you live in a rural area where you can't find people with similar interests, or you have kids, so the idea of hanging out with friends on top of working too much is laughable. If you're in either situation, use your continuing education time to connect with friends.

Begin to select your continuing education for the vibe and people rather than the course offerings. You might have two weeks of continuing education. If you do, think of taking one week for career networking and the other week for building friendships. Find out where your best friends from seminary are going, and join them. Check out online groups, and figure out the people you'd love to meet "in real life." If you long to go camping in the blazing heat with ex-evangelicals, then go there. If you love attending your seminary's annual lecture series, then sign up. If you really get into denominational politics, then go to their gatherings. If you have always wanted to attend a conference to develop your writing skills, then make that your priority. But the most important thing is to *go and meet up with the people you like.* Try to go to the same event every year and meet people you can text or call later.

Move to where your friends live. At one point in my life, I (Carol) became exhausted from developing a completely new social group every four to five years. I looked at a map of the United States. I began to think of all my friends and the people with whom I wanted to become friends. I put a mental pin in the map to see where most of them lived. When I saw that they were mostly in and around New York, I began to look for jobs in the area. Eventually I got one. Now I have my old friends and newer friends, and my life feels much richer and fuller.

Talk to neighbors and small-business owners. We can learn to go out of our way to run into people. If you can afford it, try to shop locally and go to farmers markets—places where you'll see familiar faces. Resist Amazon and self-checkout lines. Build connections at coffeehouses. Keep your headphones out of your ears and look up from your phone. The first reaction when people find out that you're a minister might be super awkward. It takes time, but soon they will begin to see you as a person beyond your vocation. Just keep talking.

Broaden your interests. Is there something that you may not be particularly interested in but is something you can share with a friend? Sometimes we don't do things because they fascinate us personally, but because we want to do something with other people. Television, sports, board games, or books may not be your thing, but if they give you a chance to have something in common with friends, then engage in them.

Meet with other pastors. You might have access to meetings that local denominational groups orchestrate. You know the ones. All the clergy go, including the tall-steeple pastor whose ego takes up all the space in the room so no one else can breathe. The retired minister shows up to berate you for not being as awesome as he was when he was serving in the parish. Or you might meet with an assigned clergy cohort in which everyone shows off and pats themselves on the back. You can't imagine sharing one authentic, honest moment with the group.

Go to those meetings anyway, and while you're there, scope out the people you *really* want to hang out with. Think about pastors, music directors, and professionals you actually like. Go to lunch. Coordinate dinners. Spend time with the people who make you laugh, and make sure you meet at least once a month. Invite spouses, and see if you can go one evening without talking about church.

Clergy from other denominations can also become good friends. They understand the quirks of the job, and you can talk honestly with them about church politics without the fear of having your remarks come back to haunt you. You might meet like-minded clergy at activist movements, vigils, or ecumenical gatherings.

Join support groups. Pastors who participate in addiction recovery often find life-giving relationships when they work through the 12 steps. Support groups can also be a huge help for overcoming grief, living with mental illness, or understanding a disease. Clergy don't have a church family we can rely on in the same way that a member does, so we need to find our support networks in other ways.

Use your time online wisely. I (Carol) have experienced the best and worst of online communities. I developed strong and meaningful friendships on social media platforms like Twitter. Also, pastors have attacked me so brutally that I couldn't even see straight by the end of the week. I tried to reason with people through my keyboard. I carefully explained the trauma that my body experienced as I responded. And then colleagues mocked me for whining, displaying cruelty that they would never have done in person. (At least, I hope they wouldn't treat people like that in person.) Social media doesn't usually expand our capacity for compassion because it's not designed to. The algorithms reward bad behavior. The social media gods amplify controversy and congratulate savagery.

If you find that social media has become a cause for constant frustration and drama, remember that the designers created it to amplify anxiety, because they know that it's good for profits.[8] Rubbernecking at the digital pileup drives revenue. Social media companies make money as we watch colleagues go bananas over ecclesial dramas, like the high-stakes issue of whether to sing Christmas carols during Advent. They keep advertisers happy as we lurk while a celebrity or pastor gets skewered. They keep their stock prices up when we digitally nail our Ninety-five Theses to the door, even when ours have less to do with simony, celibacy, and indulgences, and more to do with the fact that the denominational calendar was produced with shiny paper that's harder to write on.

While social media is a lifeline for many pastors who feel isolated in rural communities, it can also be a space where we encounter people at their worst. When studies on happiness mapped out twenty-seven leisure activities to see what made people happiest, social media ended up last on the list.[9] So use your online time wisely.

Put an unchangeable appointment on the calendar. One of the most annoying things about having clergy friends is that they quickly cancel social outings when something comes up at church. As pastors, we have flexible calendars. We often work nine-to-five, plus we make our lives available on evenings and weekends, when our parishioners are off the clock. Sometimes we become too exhausted at the end of the week to be social. We must honor an unmovable block of time for friends so we don't allow work creep to take over our lives.

Dorinda Violante literally writes "SOMETHING" on her calendar to protect her time. That way, when a parishioner asks her to meet on a Thursday night and she has Friday off, she can honestly say, "Sorry, I have SOMETHING on my calendar."

That said, we don't have to explain any of this to our parishioners. We don't have to say, "Sorry. I can't meet to talk about that $50,000 drop in pledges because I'm developing my macrame skills." It may sound superfluous to them, but they don't realize that our hobbies are actually saving our lives. A simple "no" will suffice.

Returning to Jacob

Jacob, the priest in a rural town, began to look at his friends and realized that he only had utilitarian friends inside the church. They weren't the people he could rely on through difficulties. Without such true friends, his emotional health suffered. He needed to expand his friendships, but because he lived in a town situated far away from a larger population base, there were no clergy groups, no way to organize around a hobby, and no way to get involved with activism or volunteering.

Jacob began to look for churches in a more populated area. He ended up finding a position in a suburb, close to a major city. He still had the joy of being at a small, close-knit church, but he also had access to the social support that he needed. With a short train ride, he could join pastor groups and participate in denominational events and programs. He thrived with a sizable LGBTQ community just a short distance away. When he faced difficulties in his new congregation, he could rely on a support network to get him through the difficulties.

Jacob realized that ministry can be a devastatingly lonely profession, and he was serving in that rural area at a time when people were finding it difficult to connect in general. We can learn from him. Our people are out there, and we need to find them, because we can't do this alone. When a congregation wounds us, we will need to find our support and identity in some place other than church.

Hanging out with friends allows us the space to process. We must set up our safety net before we need it.

Reflection Prompts

1. *Take a friendship inventory.* List up to ten people you feel closest to. Write down where they live and how you know them. Do you have friends who live close to you? Do you have friends outside of your family or job? Are they people you know from the internet or in the flesh? What kind of friends are they (friends for networking, friends for pleasure, and/or true friends)?

2. *Look at your time.* Do you have any intentional time that you spend with your friends? This will change with different stages of your life, but do you have time carved out in your week when you eat with a friend or group of friends? Is there a morning you can set aside to have coffee with them? Can you go on vacation or study leave with friends?

3. *Make friends.* Write down the name of a person you'd like to get to know better. Can you ask to meet that person for lunch or coffee? Can you figure out a way to meet consistently?

4. *Determine your friendship style.* Do you fuse anxiously with your friends? Do you avoid friendships? Do you use introversion as an excuse to evade social events and situations? Are there ways that you can become more secure in your friendships?

5. *Discern a potential call to friendship.* In the Bible, we see how God calls friends together—David and Jonathan, Ruth and Naomi, Jesus and Simon Peter. Do you sense that God is calling you to a covenant of friendship? What does that look like?

Chapter Three

Telling Our Story

One of the most disorienting events in the life of seminarians can happen when they read the entire Bible for the first time. When we read the text and don't skip over the parts that Sunday school avoids and the lectionary ignores, the stories rattle our faith. Sex and violence riddle the text. In each book, we encounter things that we would keep hidden in our own family histories. How did that embarrassing skeleton about Noah's drunken nakedness escape from the closet and make it into the canon?[1] Or what about Lot and his daughters?[2] We could have lived without that incest tale in our holiest book. Bathsheba starred in a brutal "me too" story, as did Dinah and Tamar, theirs being even more vicious, complete with family revenge.[3] And the early church? While pastors opine about going back to that simpler time, when we actually read the text, we find that those so-called exemplary Christians were sorting out a horrifying mix of pedophilia and slavery.[4]

It seems that in the ancient world, people told *all* the stories—the good, bad, and ugly. Some are cautionary tales, but even the heroes of the Bible have shadow sides. When writing a sacred text, why keep all of that cringeworthy content? In our churches, we try to hide things, hoping that our embarrassing histories never see the light of day. Yet there must be something powerful about the process of creating the narrative, even when it includes some shadowy details. We have a need to tell the hard parts of our stories—a burning, human need.

Daniel knew how it felt to have that consuming need after being wounded in ministry. People had always admired him. He excelled at school, his bosses gave him great reviews, and his coworkers loved him. Before he became a pastor, he rarely received a complaint on his job performance. As soon as he stepped into his new role, however, the senior pastor called him into her office every Monday to dissect and criticize everything that he had done the day before.

Now it's their weekly ritual. The senior pastor doesn't soften the blows with any praise; she just plows ahead with her list of grievances. She keeps a yellow legal notepad with a list on her desk detailing everything Daniel does wrong. He sits with his jaw clenched, trying to glean something constructive from the criticisms. She claims that anonymous people complain about his job performance. When Daniel asks for their names so he can work through the problem directly, she replies that she needs to keep those identities confidential.

Daniel never hears any negative comments from the congregation, only from the senior pastor. After a few months of this he gets suspicious. He has the feeling that he does his job *too* well. He sees the patterns. Whenever he receives public praise from anyone in the congregation, he must brace himself for the senior pastor's reaction. She becomes irritable and mean. Whenever Daniel begins to outshine his colleague, she sees it as competition for the congregation's love. He can't look too good, or she tries to force him out with continual negative pressure.

Daniel needs a place where he can release some of that pressure, where he can talk honestly. But since most of his colleagues respect the senior pastor, he can't find a friend in whom he can confide. The senior pastor is a stained-glass ceiling breaker, a respected woman in an occupation that has discriminated against women for two thousand years and counting. To utter any complaint about her feels like taking the side of the patriarchy. Plus, Daniel is almost three decades younger than her. When he has whispered any frustration to colleagues, ecclesial ageism kicks in to assume that any problem must be due to his immaturity.

Daniel longs to tell the story out loud so that he can name the issues and solve the problems. And even if he can't resolve anything, he needs the time, space, and emotional container to unburden himself. He needs a witness to his heartache.

As pastors, we know how much stories nourish people. Stories are the soul of our faith. When a man walks through suffering that never seems to end, we point him to the children of Israel wandering through the desert. When a woman feels guilty about expressing her feelings, we instruct her to read the Psalms. When a sibling needs to reconcile with a family member, we offer a reminder of the prodigal son. These stories reassure us that milk and honey await just beyond the horizon, the sacred emerges as we process our pain, and family reconciliation always lingers as a possibility. We not only need to hear these ancient accounts in themselves, but they also point to our need to be able to tell our own stories to someone who stops to listen to us, acknowledges our heartache, and witnesses our suffering. In the healing process, the stories will help us to define ourselves, understand our reactive emotions, and reveal our theology.

What Stories Can Do

Stories Help Us to Define Ourselves

Processing our stories requires us to determine how much other people define them. On a daily basis, we typically hear positive and negative definitions of who we are. One of your parishioners may tell you at the end of worship that you are a wonderful preacher. You may also hear from a spouse that you need to stop being so passive-aggressive. Or you might hear from a pharmaceutical ad that your eczema should make you ashamed. We could decide that all the positive qualities attributed to us are true and the negative ones are simply a misunderstanding. That might help pacify our fragile emotional psyches, but ultimately it isn't very constructive. We need to determine who we are through our own self-exploration—the good and not-so-good qualities we possess.

This is where the friendships we have developed come into play. True friends listen to our stories, and through questions, humor, and correction they reject our paranoid rants and right-size our grandiosity. They celebrate with us and keep us accountable. Good friends have keen BS detectors, and they aren't afraid to use them. The back-and-forth of storytelling between friends helps us to gain a clearer perspective of who we are and who we are not. True friends tell us when we're wrong and when we're right. They tell us to change our actions when we need to. Having these kinds of friends helps us to see how we project ourselves to others. They act like an honest mirror that reflects back to us what others see. Sometimes we don't have friends like this, or maybe we want to check their honesty, so we call in a professional like a therapist, a life coach, or a family systems coach.

Understanding how others see us is only the first step in this process of self-definition. The next step is identifying our core beliefs. Our core beliefs distinguish us and influence what we say and do. Some of these might be easy to jot down on paper, but others might take months or years to determine. As we tell our stories to friends, we also convey our deepest-held beliefs. In our conversations, as they reflect back our truth or misconceptions, we realize our core. We might think that we have a core belief that all people are good. So how do we live that out? How does that core belief influence our thoughts about homeless people? Abortion? Homosexuality?

Grace is a pastor who affirms a core belief that "people are good, regardless of their race, gender, or sexual identity." She considers herself a progressive Christian serving in a progressive United Methodist congregation. Two women who regularly attend the church ask Grace to officiate their wedding. She agrees, but then she has doubts about her decision. She discusses the situation with a friend, examining the different aspects of the story. Her denomination doesn't allow lesbian weddings, and she worries that her officiating will cause problems. She also frets about what some of the parishioners will think. Although the congregation is progressive, not everyone agrees with breaking the rules of the denomination. She then wonders what her parents would say. Grace grew up in a conservative church in the South, and although she became more and more progressive, her parents didn't.

The more she shares her story, the more Grace realizes that she finds it difficult to live out this core belief. As she navigates her friend's reaction, she begins to wonder, "Is this truly a core belief I have, or is it simply one I aspire to have?"

That is a difficult question for any of us to answer. Talking through this challenging part of our story and asking the people we trust the most what they think helps us reflect further on our core beliefs and how we live them out. This circular process is truly a lifelong development of getting to know who we are and working to live that out each and every day. This is the process of writing the story of who we are. In Bowen theory we call this self-differentiation.[5]

Stories Help Us Make Sense of Our Trauma Triggers

In addition to defining ourselves, telling our stories helps us to understand why we might become reactive in certain situations.[6] Sometimes unhealthy people in congregations have an uncanny and unconscious ability to sense the trauma that we have endured and hurt us with it. Whether they do it consciously or not, they seem to know just how to push our buttons. That's what happened to Edwin.

Edwin, a pastor in a small church, grew up with a mother who emotionally abused him. He never had a chance to process the pain of his childhood or feel a sense of safety in his adulthood. Then a woman in his congregation became addicted to pain medication. One night she called him after midnight. He answered because she lived alone, and he thought she might be in some physical danger. But when he greeted her, her slurred and mocking tone indicated that she was under the influence of the opioids. His eyes widened as he listened to her.

"I am so disappointed in you," she spewed the moment he answered. "I had hopes when you became our pastor. I really did. But you have been terrible. You don't care about me. You don't care about our congregation. I don't even know why you became a pastor."

Her poisonous diatribe continued. Fumbling a quick excuse, Edwin immediately got off the phone. When he poked the screen to hang up, his hands were shaking so much that the phone slid from his grasp and fell on the floor. He looked down at it, as if it had turned into a deadly viper.

In the next few months, Edwin fell into a deep depression, allowing the abuse to penetrate his soul. He knew that this church member was not in her right mind when she said those things. He understood that she probably didn't even remember that she had called him. But the words paralyzed him, and he didn't understand why.

Edwin began seeing a therapist. When he finally had the chance to tell his story, he realized that his congregant had used the exact same words his mother had used to berate him when he was growing up.

Sometimes we react to a situation with intense fear, anger, or depression that seems outsized for the issue at hand. Internal alarm bells clang fiercely. Our response is not necessarily because of the event itself, but because the situation immediately transports us to a similar time when we didn't have the emotional tools and understanding we needed. We may have responded with fear or rage, and we fall into that same outsized response when the memory surfaces.

When we have intense reactions due to past trauma, we should stop and take deep breaths.[7] In the middle of the situation, when we suddenly feel that electric current of frustration running through our bodies, changing our breathing patterns can help us regulate our emotions. Then we can find a therapist or counselor to help us process the experience. Being able to tell our stories in a safe, confidential space will help us release some of the anxiety. We gain power in the situation by drawing connections between our heightened emotional state and past events. We can construct word containers for our unruly feelings.

Compare the process to watching a terrible disease overtake someone without knowing the cause. When we discover a diagnosis, a label for the illness, we feel a greater sense of control. It's the same way with our emotional life. When we can label the pain with words, understand its origin, and construct a narrative structure that makes sense of our chaos, we regain some sense of emotional regulation.

Stories Inform Our Theology

As pastors, we also need to realize how stories inform our theology. This is different from determining our core beliefs because it has more to do with what we teach and preach, while our core beliefs have to do with our identity. Many of us were able to go through deconstruction during seminary, but we may still find ourselves praying to a harsh and judgmental being who is just waiting for us to screw up. As we go through traumatic events, growth happens when we can begin to understand God in light of the trauma. Often our spiritual understandings will evolve, and our stories help to reveal and inform those changes.

Rosa realized that she harbored toxic theology in her stories when she began to go through a drawn-out church conflict. She began waking up each morning with an overwhelming sense of guilt. She had grown up in a conservative evangelical church where she was constantly told she was a sinner, deserving of damnation. She went to seminary and served United Church of Christ congregations with more loving views of God and humanity, but when crises occurred, her automatic reaction was to reach for those awful assumptions. She could not shake that shameful dread in her gut, even after her theology became healthier in her head.

When Rosa told the story of her church wounds, she often revealed her belief in divine punishment. "I'm not sure what I did to deserve such a difficult call!" In her quick joke, she implied that God wanted her to suffer as some sort of punishment.

When we tell our story, it's also important to listen and to think about the beliefs behind our words. What sort of story are we telling about ourselves? About God? If we focus on our failings and express self-hatred, we need to reexamine our theology. Likewise, if the story features a God who desires to hurt or destroy us, or is anything less than loving, we will want to excavate our story in light of a more compassionate and loving theology. This healthy theology will be particularly important as we develop our story and use it to make meaning. (We'll cover that more in chapter 8.)

How Stories Die

Unfortunately, we don't all have the same capacity for storytelling. We might have grown up in a culture that prized a good narrative, and so we learned how to craft a plot at an early age. We might have great friends who will listen to our frustrations. Or we might have been formed within a family that valued silent fortitude and so we don't have a lot of friends who listen. When our stories meet resistance, we stiffen our upper lips. Without a thought, we walk away and never have a chance to process what's happened to us. If our stories get shut down regularly, we need to understand how our stories die so that we can resist the patterns. When we've been wounded, the necessity of storytelling becomes so strong that when we don't handle our stories with care, we can internalize them, morph them, or react to them.[8]

We Swallow Our Stories with Stoicism

Pastors can be incredibly ascetic. We often endure the pain of our call with exquisite grace. But that outer dignity can come at a price, creating massive inner turmoil. When we suppress our emotions, we can internalize the things that people say about us.

The stories don't go away. Instead, we store the resentment in our bellies. Then the swallowed dramas boil. The uncomfortable steam of emotions tries to find another release valve, often giving us high blood pressure, irritable bowels, or other stress reactions. We might respond to the pressure by numbing it—drinking too much, eating too much, or engaging in other self-destructive behaviors.

One pastor confided to us that she didn't have any support at her job and had no outlet to tell her story. Eventually, her neck muscles became so tight that they curved her cervical spine in the opposite direction of what was normal and healthy.

We Choke Out Our Stories with Toxic Positivity

When God calls us to a particular church and people in that congregation begin to attack us, it's difficult to make sense of the paradox: God loves us, God wants us to have an abundant life, and the church God called us to is slowly killing us.

So we pretend that the third thing is not happening. We ignore the bombs exploding around us. Then when we can no longer ignore them, we try to morph the situation into something positive.

For example, Jasmine had a couple of good friends she could talk with whenever the stresses of her job became too much. Yet each time she began to tell them the truth of her situation, she interrupted herself and said, "But it's all good." She was a positive person who hated to complain. She didn't want her friends to think she was a whiner, so any time she hit a sour note, she immediately changed her tune, explaining how grateful she was for what she had.

At the end of the night when the friends left, Jasmine felt intensely lonely, like no one in the world understood her. The truth was, Jasmine barely knew herself. Even when she wrote in her journal or prayed, she never allowed herself to acknowledge her difficulties. She littered her speech with optimistic clichés. She was skipping through the valley of the shadow of death with a blindfold on. She morphed the reality, pretended everything was okay, until she got ill. Finally, the optimistic denial caught up with Jasmine and she had to spend a couple of weeks in the hospital. In that hospital bed, she faced her reality. Even though she had tried to change her story into something positive, her body knew the truth of her situation.

Homeostasis Seekers Will Stomp on Our Stories

As we begin to write our stories, we'll have friends, family, and colleagues who will try to erase them. They'll have different motives for this. For some, it's a misguided form of protection. They want the pain to go away, so they try to force the story to go away. Or they might have a drive to defend the institution they serve, wanting to maintain homeostasis at all costs.[9]

Benjamin experienced this when he sat with his colleagues at a continuing education event. There was a lecture, and then the participants broke up into small groups to discuss the issues that had been presented. Benjamin mustered up the courage to talk about the devastating racism that he endured at church and in the denomination. In return, his (white) colleagues responded with cringey religious platitudes:

> "Look at the bright side!"
> "All things work together for good."
> "God has a plan."

Then the white pastors proceeded to brag about all of the civil rights activities they had been involved in throughout the decades, declaring that "not all pastors" in their denomination were racist. Benjamin struggled to suppress his eye-rolling.

When faced with the shame of discrimination and their part in it, Benjamin's colleagues could not affirm his pain, nor could they look at institutional structures and how they could change. Instead, their energy went into maintaining homeostasis. They protected the organization's behavior by silencing Benjamin's discomfort and insisting that the situation wasn't as bad as he thought. They used religious language and cheerful expressions, trying to soothe Benjamin by transforming his suffering into some sort of collateral damage that served a divine plan. As they boasted about their marching and protesting, they shifted the focus from Benjamin's pain to their antiracism work. They whitewashed his story by making themselves the main characters and ignoring Benjamin. All of this left Benjamin feeling angry and annoyed.

Likewise, bishops, presbyters, district superintendents, and committees on ministry all want the church to succeed. They may be tasked to help with pastoral relations, and they usually understand that healthy pastors help create healthy churches. But their ultimate allegiance often lies with the structure they serve, even when that organization is unjust. Even if they don't overtly take the "side" of the church, they know that when a pastor leaves a church setting, the congregation remains and continues to be their responsibility, so their default mode is to maintain homeostasis. Even if the status quo wasn't working for anyone, they long to return to it.

Institutions Will Use Legal Maneuvers to Quiet Stories

Institutions and organizations also employ nondisclosure agreements (NDAs) to kill stories and protect themselves. When a pastor has been forced to leave a congregation, she might be told she must sign an NDA in order to receive a severance package. Since ministers are not often eligible for unemployment benefits, a firing often puts the pastor in a horrible financial situation. So she signs. Or she decides to keep the story secret in order to preserve her status.

This legal maneuver to hush people up and protect reputations can have devastating effects on pastors *and* congregations. If the pastor has done something wrong, it allows her to go to another church and repeat her behavior. These documents have allowed predators involved in chronic sexual misconduct to be shuffled from one church to another, without any consequence, endangering more people.

If the pastor has not done anything wrong, it subjects her to the whim of powerful church members, who often step out of the denominational system and hire the type of lawyers that the pastor could never afford. Pastors can be fired without cause, and then they have no recourse because they had to sign the NDA. NDAs can create a culture where powerful bullies indiscriminately run the church and punish those who don't give them or their families enough deference.

The legal maneuver also leaves the congregation and the pastor with no ability to deal with the emotional turmoil that they have just endured. The story reverberates through the congregation, except it gets twisted with rumors and innuendo. Likewise, the pastor has no chance to tell her story and process what happened, so that crucial ingredient for healing is absent.

As we become more aware of our personal and systemic tendencies to hide the drama, we can find safer places to open up. We can focus on how to process what's happened to us.

How to Tell Our Stories

Find a Story Holder

I (Carol) have a friend who is in no way connected to the church. He is deeply spiritual but rarely steps into a sanctuary on Sunday mornings. I love telling him my professional woes. He is quick to respond with jokes laced with curse words and name calling. I know that one of the most helpful books on coping with difficult people is titled *Never Call Them Jerks*, and I do take that advice to heart.[10] But sometimes I can laugh and detach a bit when I hear *someone else* call them jerks. A profane response jars me into realizing how enmeshed I am in my role as a pastor. My nonreligious friend has allowed a helpful release and a lot of amusement over the years.

Many pastors have a story holder, someone who will listen to them with care, focus, and attention. It is often beneficial to find someone completely outside the church world to help us process and gain perspective. Or we can work with a therapist or spiritual director. Some clergy report that going through EMDR (eye movement desensitization and reprocessing) treatment as they tell their stories has been extremely therapeutic.

There are also times when our storytelling doesn't involve another person. We can set aside a time to pray and (if it's possible) find a space to pray out loud. Even telling our story to a book can help. The psychologists Richard G. Tedeschi and Lawrence Calhoun found that journaling for twenty minutes a day can help people process their emotions when they're going through difficulties. It can help them experience growth in gratitude, relationships, possibilities, strength, and spirituality.[11]

We must add a caution here. With the ubiquity of the internet, we can get a quick release and affirmation through tweeting or posting on Facebook. Our dopamine rises when a crowd of friends and followers support and praise us. Their response might lure us into thinking of social media as a safe space. But the truth is that we never know who's watching and reading. Pastors have faced printouts of their own tweets at personnel meetings or as they negotiated their terms of employment. When we publish things for the world to see, we must be prepared for the whole world to see them.

In addition, we can't always be vulnerable with everyone. Especially if we're part of a group of people that has been historically discriminated against, we need to be careful about whom we offer our stories to.[12]

Whatever form our story holder may take, it is important to bear witness to what we have endured. Whether it is a professional, a group of friends, or a trusted colleague, this witness can surround us and hear our pain. We may want to engage in some sort of ritual to help process the pain. Ministry leaders often focus on words, but we hold trauma in our whole bodies. As we understand and process our stories, we will want to pay attention to all the ways we can express what's happened—physically, spiritually, and artistically. We can pay attention to what's happening in our bodies, the searing pain in our gut, the annoying twitch of our eye, or the piercing headache that crawls up from our spine.

While our religious responses to negative emotions often focus on dismissing them with annoying platitudes, avoiding our emotions rarely works. Instead, we need to find a way to feel the anger and hatred in order to let go of it. Here are some practices pastors shared that helped them to process.

Write out the story and ritually destroy it. Put nasty emails through a sacred shredder. Create a bonfire with a couple of friends, and burn your story. One time I (Carol) put a particularly toxic annual review in a dump outside of town. As I dropped the paper into a giant hole in the ground, I thought of Gehenna, a fiery garbage dump situated in a narrow valley outside of Jerusalem's walls. When it's referred to in the Scriptures, scholars often translate the place as "hell." As I watched the review become buried by more filth, I let go of my heartache.

Make some sort of artwork. If you're not someone who likes to draw or paint, you can always collage. Get some good old-fashioned paper magazines. Rip out colors, words, and images that stir you. Glue them down and reflect on what the words and images say to your situation. When you are done, journal what you see. You can keep your creation or destroy it. The point is not to create an amazing piece of art; it is to allow your whole body and brain to feel the depths of the emotion as well as the comforts that follow.

Find a vigorous release. Physical activity can help us process complex negativity. If you are able, exercise, garden, do woodworking, or find another form of strenuous play. Or you may want to sign up for Habitat for Humanity or a service project.

Make sure that you have space to cry, scream, and get furious. It may be socially unacceptable for us as pastors to give voice to our full range of emotions, especially if we live in a small-town fishbowl where everyone watches us. The way people misinterpret even the most benign emotional response can have a lot to do with our age ("immature"), gender ("hysterical"), or race ("angry"). When Ashley was a young pastor, well-meaning colleagues often admonished her to "grow thicker skin." Then after years of therapy, she realized that her biggest challenge was feeling her emotions, not deflecting them. The advice was based on her age and gender, rather than the situation and circumstance.

We can't neglect to process our complicated feelings, even when they come with an embodied response. We can find a space. For example, pastors reported that they could yell when they hiked or cry when they showered.

Returning to Daniel

Daniel continues to have difficulty navigating the relationship with his senior pastor. The weekly lists of complaints only seem to get longer. At the same time, issues are developing at home, and his marriage is in trouble. Daniel feels that his wife doesn't support him enough, considering the stress he endures at work, and places too many "demands" on him. He feels criticized at work and at home.

Daniel begins looking for a new job. He's done with the church and determines that pastoring just isn't for him. But what jobs are available for someone with a master of divinity degree? He looks at chaplain positions, nonprofits, and even positions in denominational agencies. Nothing excites him, and they all seem like an escape. Yet he continues through the process, hoping it will give him peace.

At the same time, a friend recommends a therapist to Daniel. Through therapy, Daniel tells his story and learns to define himself beyond how his senior pastor describes him. This helps Daniel to realize that the problem isn't ministry in general; it's the difficult relationship he has with the senior pastor. With the therapist's help, he tries to change the dynamic that exists between them, and their communication improves, but the senior pastor ultimately can't do away with the complaint list, insisting it's for Daniel's improvement as a pastor.

Daniel applies for other church positions, all at the senior pastor level. A new church calls him that is smaller than his current church, but he'll be the only pastor. It proves to be a very good fit, and Daniel thrives in this new setting. It certainly isn't perfect, but his anxiety level is greatly reduced.

Outside perspectives can help us and keep us grounded, but as Daniel learned, sometimes they can be toxic. With the help of a therapist Daniel defined who he is, recognized his gifts as a pastor, and realized that the work gave him great fulfillment. He also learned that the systemic problems we face at work commonly also surface at home (and vice versa). At first Daniel thought that his wife's criticism confirmed that he was failing both at church and at home. As he explored this more, he learned that because of his treatment by the senior pastor, he was extra sensitive to anything that might seem like criticism. What he thought was criticism from his wife simply wasn't.

When we have a chance to tell our stories, we gain greater understanding of our context—an important next step in our journey toward health.

Reflection Prompts

1. *Journal for twenty minutes a day for six weeks.* If this makes you twenty minutes late for the office, see if you can negotiate for the time. It may be more important for the health of your ministry than appeasing clock watchers. You might want to journal as a Lent or Advent practice. Remember, studies show that twenty minutes of daily journaling can help you heal and grow.

2. *List your story holders.* Look at your list. If you have friends who are not great listeners, or if your situation is more complex than a friend with a compassionate ear can handle, consider hiring a professional. Clergy often have good insurance that covers mental health.

3. *Explore alternative storytelling.* Are there forms that your story can take other than verbal expressions? Can you draw, paint, or collage? Do you play music or dance? Romans 8:26 talks about how the Spirit prays with us with wordless groans. What would that look like in your life? Using alternative forms of expression often can reveal a great deal to us.

4. *Work on differentiation.* Finish the following sentences as quickly as you can and without thinking deeply about them. If a question doesn't apply to your situation, then skip it.

My partner thinks that I am _____.

My family thinks that I am _____.

My parents think that I am _____.

My friends think that I am _____.

Some people in my church think that I am _____.

Other people in my church think that I am _____.

I remember when someone described me as _____.

I felt like a person really understood me when they said that I was _____.

I think that I am _____.

I feel most like myself when I am _____.

I don't feel like myself when _____.

Look at your answers. What resonates with the person God has called you to be? What descriptions sound authentic and true? Can you see your shadow side in the descriptions? When were people completely wrong about who you are? Do your actions match who you think you are?

5. *Focus on the "why."* As you tell your story, identify the who, the what, and the where. Then really concentrate on the why. If you are working with a friend, have that person ask you, "Why?" If you're not with a friend, ask yourself three to five times so that you can get through the layers and to the heart of the matter. For example:

Why did you get so angry when he scolded you?
Because I felt humiliated.
Why did you feel humiliated?
It made me feel like a child.
Why did it remind you of being a child?

Chapter Four

Identifying Our Context

Chloe became aware of her turmoil when the pain of stress seared her gut. But it took a crisis for her to understand that the way she functioned in her context helped to create the reaction. Before the pandemic, Chloe deftly juggled all the jobs in her life. Then COVID spread and her two children suddenly began homeschooling. Her husband set up an office in the basement. And Chloe put together a makeshift study in the dining room.

Chloe worked as the solo pastor of a church whose members represented a broad spectrum of political beliefs. At first the congregation functioned well, with members looking out for each other's health and safety. But as the months wore on and the political tension in the country heightened, the factions in the church grew as well. Some members wanted to meet in person, while others wanted to worship exclusively online. Disagreements over whether or not to wear a mask became a flashpoint for anger and frustration, fueled by rhetoric at the national level, which became so harsh that a politician compared mandatory mask-wearing to forced encampment during the Holocaust.[1] The isolated members of the church spread toxic rhetoric through social media and drove a wedge through the congregation. Since they no longer had a chance to meet up for coffee hour or potlucks, they never had a chance to rehumanize one another. Chloe had previously been able to navigate the tricky red-blue divide in her congregation, but as the pandemic wore on, her role as a purple church pastor became more difficult.

Chloe soldiered on. She stepped into a caretaker role at church as well as at home. She gracefully moderated complaints, heard different sides, and negotiated compromises. At home, she attended to her children and facilitated their needs as online students. She also continued to manage the household cleaning, shopping, and cooking. Although her husband helped with certain chores, Chloe had the responsibility of assigning tasks, negotiating eyerolls, and completing duties. His job paid more, and hers had more flexibility. Chloe began to work around her husband's office hours, space, and needs.

On the good days, Chloe felt like a superpastor, competent and on top of things. When she learned to manage streaming technologies for worship and meetings, she felt proud of her newfound abilities. On the bad days, Chloe wasn't sure how much longer she could keep it together. She made so much room for everyone else that she didn't have any room for herself. Her body began to wear with strain. She only had twenty-four hours in a day, so when her children's school tasks began to take up more time, she gave up her exercise routine and worked late into the night on church duties.

Because of COVID restrictions, she started buying groceries online instead of going to the farmers market, which had been one of her favorite activities each week. The pandemic robbed her of other personal joys as well, such as going to the hair salon. She missed the indulgence of a shampoo and scalp massage. Taking time for simple pleasures like a long bath or a fancy latte at a coffeehouse suddenly seemed like a distant memory.

Chloe lost weight. The stress stole her appetite. Her eye began to twitch. Her stomach either housed a heavy rock of dread or fought with an acute searing pain. Chloe was no stranger to pain. Due to a childhood illness, she had learned to ignore discomfort. So when her body began to give her warnings, she simply pretended the ache didn't exist and trudged forward.

Then an elder sent a long email to the personnel committee complaining that the pastor wasn't doing her job. The email contained a long list of minute things that Chloe had left undone. Plus, this elder wanted to know why she had not called every member of the congregation to check up on them. The personnel committee, which didn't fully understand or appreciate the monumental task of moving worship and Christian education online, brought the man's concern with some additional queries to Chloe. Chloe wanted to defend herself and explain that the crisis had brought many new demands and required a shift in priorities, but she had no strength to respond. The criticisms almost broke her.

Chloe had been thrust into the roles of caretaker for her family, supervisor of her children's education, manager of her household, and administrator of her church. Stoically, she had taken up every extra job the crisis produced. Now she didn't have anything left. The litany of complaints felt like a wake of vultures picking her bones dry. Exhaustion overtook her. She became sick, and for the next two weeks she could barely get out of bed.

As she finally rested, Chloe became aware of the emotional systems that she worked in and realized how she responded to them.

Thinking Systemically

We live in multiple emotional systems. Your family is an emotional system. Your church is an emotional system. Any group of individuals who work, live, or are in any way organized to be together forms an emotional system. But what is a system? We can't see or touch it. Yet it has an enormous impact on us. We use metaphors and analogies to describe systems.

- A system is like an old-fashioned clock. We turn like gears and components, each working in connection with others. We act and react based on the actions and reactions of others.
- Virginia Satir describes a system as a mobile: "If the wires on one of the pieces of the mobile are twisted, the mobile would spin improperly. Instead of a delicately balanced mobile, each piece would get entangled and out of balance at the slightest breeze."[2]
- The Bible uses a body metaphor: "For just as the body is one and has many members, and all the members of the body, though many, are one body, so it is with Christ" (1 Cor. 12:12).

These incomplete analogies help us understand that individually we function as parts and that together we form a whole emotional system.

As a family therapist, I (James) am often asked to see a child in a family who is having "problems." The child acts out and needs to see someone who can help him figure out what's wrong and fix it. An individual model of therapy focuses on the child and tries to understand what is wrong with him. A systems model of therapy understands that the child in therapy is not the problem. He is a symptom of the problem, which resides in the system. Almost always, people behave badly not because there is something wrong with them. Instead, they react poorly to pressures surrounding them.

What does this look like in a church? It might look like Ed, a man in his late seventies who serves on the board of his local congregation. In the middle of a discussion about the budget, Ed starts yelling at the pastor, Jaylen, seemingly for no reason. Ed says that Jaylen manages money incompetently and blames him for all the church's financial issues. Jaylen yells back, defending his work and blaming Ed for failing to run an effective stewardship campaign. This continues for several minutes until Ed storms out of the meeting.

From a system's view, is Ed the problem? Does he need anger management classes? Well, maybe. Or we can think systemically and see how, like gears on a clock, Ed turns in timely reaction to other forces beyond his control:

- Maybe this outburst grew out of previous interactions with Jaylen. The intensity has escalated over many encounters.
- Maybe the flare-up came from Ed's job. Ed works for the family business, and his younger sister has told him that the family wants him to have a smaller role in the company.
- Maybe the eruption originated from the declining health of Ed's wife, who suffers from pancreatic cancer.
- Or maybe Ed's anger resulted from a combination of all these situations and more.

Systems thinking helps us to see the interconnectedness of our relationships. Our experiences and the experiences of those connected to us produce reactions within us. We feel good when those around us feel good, and we feel sad when those around us are sad. Most significantly, we feel anxious when those around us are anxious.

As we explore the context (the church), we first need to dig deeper into our understanding of anxiety and the greatest driver of anxiety for the church—survival. We then must work through several important systems concepts that help us understand how the system operates.

Anxiety

We know when anxiety overcomes us. A grey cloud lingers, so we walk around like a doomed kid perpetually on the way to the principal's office—only we don't know exactly what we did wrong. Or anxious thoughts poke us awake in the middle of the night, preventing us from drifting back to sleep. Or we might have a physical reaction—an overcaffeinated feeling causes our hand to shake, our eye to twitch, or our stomach to tie into knots.

We recognize anxiety, but how do we know when we have more anxiety than we can handle? Wouldn't it be great if we could get a reading on our Fitbit that told us our anxiety score? Of course, we would also need a score that indicated how much anxiety we can tolerate. We cannot quantify anxiety, so how do we determine how much stress and anxiety exist at any moment in our lives?

Our daily anxiety comes in two varieties: acute and chronic. Acute, or situational, anxiety comes from the stresses of life. You've seen the stress tests in magazines and BuzzFeed articles:

- 10 points for buying a house,
- 20 points for getting married, or
- 40 points for the death of a spouse.

These tests reveal that anxiety is additive. The more stressful events that take place in our lives, the higher the score and the more we feel the anxiety.

Another type of anxiety is chronic. When we experience things in our society and community that are out of our control, it causes chronic anxiety. These disruptions can be situational in nature, but they have an impact that is far greater than us or our families. A financial crisis can easily lead to a spike in chronic anxiety. As churches in our denominations close, we wonder how long our congregation can survive, and that awareness increases our chronic anxiety. A global pandemic like COVID caused a huge increase in worldwide chronic anxiety. Without a clear ending to these disasters, anxiety grows and leads to a mental health crisis.

Chronic anxiety is simply our baseline for the level of worry that we walk around with every day. Even if we maintained stress-free lives in terms of personal events, chronic anxiety would still be there. Other sources of chronic anxiety include:

- a volatile political climate,
- systemic racism,
- global climate change,
- gun violence, and
- our own mortality.

All of these and more impact us daily. We may "ignore" some stressors until the next news cycle reminds us of them. But unfortunately, we live in a world in which so many stressors exist that unless we completely disconnect from hearing anything about global events, we will be impacted by them.

In our churches, we may experience the growing cost of ministry gradually overtaking our diminishing resources, which causes chronic anxiety. In contrast, the largest pledging family moving out of state this year causes acute anxiety. The chronic anxiety of diminishing resources compounds the acute anxiety of the loss of the family.

When anxiety (both chronic and acute) runs high in the church system, several indicators appear. We can detect the same warning signs in individuals, but in a system, the alert spreads beyond one or two individuals and becomes an alarm ringing throughout many in the congregation.

First, we find significant reactivity. This means that a person reacts with greater intensity than we would expect for the situation, as when Ed erupted with fury at Jaylen over finances. Ed's over-the-top emotions made everyone shake their heads and wonder, "What is going on here?" That is reactivity. Of course, reactivity isn't always as obvious as that example. A person who begins to tear up when someone discusses seating arrangements for a wedding reception is clearly emotionally fueled by something else.

Second, when the system is anxious, polarization occurs. People plant themselves on one side of an issue, and anyone who does not remain firmly on their side becomes an enemy. In our current national climate this happens more and more, which signals that the chronic anxiety in our society remains very high. Polarization divides people and allows for reactivity to flow toward those who stand against us.

I (James) am part of a denomination (the United Methodist Church) that has been ripping itself apart for decades. As a denomination, we have pastors and congregations who affirm the LGBTQ community, and we have pastors and congregations who affirm the church's official position that "homosexuality is incompatible with Christian teaching."[3] For decades we lived with this tension. In the last few years, the polarization has pushed the denomination to the point of fracture as congregations have exited. It is not a coincidence that this has happened at the same time as our political and social order has become polarized in so many ways—over Black Lives Matter, women's health, and general partisanship.

Finally, we lose almost all flexibility in a highly anxious system. In the same way polarization leads us to black-and-white thinking, a rigid decision-making process emerges that doesn't allow for compromise. Again, we see this in our own context as lawmakers dig in and fail to make compromises on important issues.

Isabel recognized a lack of flexibility when faced with a budget shortfall in her church. Giving decreased during the pandemic, so she worked to cut some line items. A couple of people in the congregation wanted to cut a valued employee. The church had many creative options available—utilizing rental space, asking members for more money, or hosting a fundraiser. But they got caught in the rigid gridlock of binary thinking, focused on whether or not to keep the employee.

When Isabel attempted to be logical and point out the various options, she failed. When she tried to be rational, she could not be heard. Finally, she had to recognize the systemic anxiety and understand that rigid emotions dominated the body, not flexible rationality. So she focused on decreasing the anxiety instead of just trying to figure out what to do about the employee.

Survival

The system itself can also heighten anxiety levels. A family system has one primary function: survival. When we understand a congregation as a family system, we realize that the system is formed out of its relationships. Any perceived danger to the congregation (e.g., financial strain, attendance decrease, or leadership transition) threatens the relational structure and the survival of the system.

This explains why church conflicts become so intense. Mainline churches have lurched on the edge of survival for many years, and a global pandemic that required social distancing made things worse. When a church moves closer to closure (or to losing its pastor), the anxiety level increases significantly along with the reactivity in the congregation.

For instance, Maya was appointed to serve a newly formed church made up of two congregations that had decided to merge. Everything was going as planned. The new congregation spent several months worshiping in one building, then they switched and worshiped for several months in the other building. During the first year, Maya and the trustees studied the structures and locations in order to make a recommendation on which building to use. Then it came time for the newly formed church to vote. Many people turned out. Maya and the trustees recommended the smaller congregation's building. They communicated well-presented and rational reasons for their choice.

An explosive and emotional discussion followed. The eruption sounded nothing like a church meeting. The anger that flared up from those who had come from the larger congregation horrified Maya. They attacked her personally. They insisted she had rigged the whole process just to get what she wanted. It was painful and abusive. When the vote was taken, the larger congregation defeated the smaller one. Maya wondered how they would ever become one church.

Though the attacks were personal, the fury had roots in something that had nothing to do with Maya. They erupted from the fear of those from the larger congregation that they would not survive. The ensuing vote was not based on logic or rationality, but on the need for things to stay the same for the largest number of people. It was a vote to maintain homeostasis.

Homeostasis

The escalation in survival anxiety brings the system back to homeostasis. Imagine the church as a rubber band. Every time we seek to change the system, we pull on the band. The more we try to change the system, the more intense the resistance. The band's natural position is homeostasis. Homeostasis may not maintain a perfect harmony in which everything operates smoothly, but it works "to preserve the organizational principles of its existence."[4]

Consider a declining downtown church that used to be considered a "tall steeple church" in its glory days. Now it has an aging congregation and a pastor who is nearing retirement with many medical issues. Although plenty of congregants are willing to make decisions to manage the upkeep of the building, very few can do the work themselves. Don has the motivation and the time to roll up his sleeves and do the labor. He also obstructs things. He insists that the trustees should pay to have the church's silver Communion set locked up properly, because he doesn't like that the church kept it on display in the hallway. The other trustees refuse.

So Don steals the silver. After several weeks he brings it back, saying that he found it in an alley. The trustees install locks on the cabinet the next week. The other trustees know Don took the Communion set, and they could confront him about his actions, but they ask themselves, "If he left, who would repair the church appliances for free? Who would set the thermostats for winter?"

This is homeostasis. It isn't peaceful or anxiety free. But it works.[5]

Multigenerational Projection Process

Homeostasis extends before and beyond our present generation. Murray Bowen calls this phenomenon the Multigenerational Projection Process.[6] The powerful force of homeostasis keeps the system remarkably similar from generation to generation. Our response feels personal and independent, but when we take a step back, we see that it often repeats through the generations. A certain occupation might run in the family. Coping strategies such as alcohol abuse will be passed down from parent to child to grandchild. Or extreme versions of the Multigenerational Projection Process might include suicides that repeat through the generations.

Congregations operate like families and live out these same principles. Understanding the stories of the congregations we serve becomes vital. We need to go beyond reading the commemorative book with a five-page history followed by a collection of recipes that someone put together. We need to speak with some of the oldest members and get the real account. We can ask about the scandals and the conflicts. Most importantly, we can find out how people responded to them. This will help us to recognize how the congregation operates and how we should respond.

If a church has unresolved trauma in its history (e.g., a pastor who stole money, a sex scandal, or an act of violence), the trauma from that event lives in the organization. When no one explores, processes, or heals from the distress, a reactive, illogical, or overly emotional response can surprise us. In the same way that a past assault might trigger fear in one person, the organization also responds to trauma with distress.

When this happens, it can cause confusion, because sometimes the people who react don't understand their heightened emotions. And a *really strange* thing? The person participating in these corporate PTSD behaviors may not even know about the original event.

Technical versus Adaptive Leadership

Another important tool to understand a system is learning the difference between technical and adaptive change. Ron Heifetz introduced the need for adaptive leadership to affect change in an organization.[7] Technical leadership uses the knowledge and means that we currently possess to seek change. Assuming we understand the problem, technical leaders just need to fix the solution at hand. It can feel like using a screwdriver to hammer in a nail. Church leaders often come up with technical fixes:

- Adding screens and projectors into worship to attract young people to church,
- Requiring pastors to log and share all pastoral visits because of a lack of trust,
- Approving a ten-page job description in response to questions of pastoral effectiveness,
- Hiring a young pastor to bring in young families, or
- Conducting a survey to solve personnel issues.

We could go on for hours, listing dozens of meaningless acts that attempt to placate someone for a short time. What they all have in common is that they are a solution that simply doesn't address the underlying problem.

We need to develop solutions only after we truly understand the problem at hand. This may seem easy, but it isn't. When church leaders question a pastor about how many pastoral visits she makes, it indicates that they don't trust the pastor. They don't believe the pastor can make decisions about whom to contact. They worry about how the pastor divides labor and uses time. They fear the pastor will kill the church. No one needs a log. It won't solve the problem. Instead, the pastor and members need to focus on the adaptive solution—building trust.

I (James) consulted with the leadership of a struggling congregation. Executives and their growing families had once populated the pews, but now the church was fighting for survival. One presenting problem was the church's difficulty finding volunteers to host coffee hour. When I asked more about that, I was told that for each coffee hour, the volunteers had to bring out all the fine china and silverware. Setting it all up and washing it afterward was a significant task. When I asked if they could host coffee hour without china and silverware, it was as if I had asked them to burn their church organ. Changing approaches, I asked, "What is the purpose of a coffee hour?" And I received several responses:

> "Time for the congregation to have fellowship."
> "A way to encourage people to stay for the adult education program."
> "An opportunity to show off our china."

Everyone laughed.

They didn't mention anything about visitors or hospitality. We began to have a long conversation in which we discussed questions like these: What purpose should coffee hour serve? Why should we have it? What does it mean to be hospitable? Do we want it? What do we need to make that happen? No one answered that they needed the china or silverware. They talked about establishing a group to explore deeper how they could focus on hospitality and use the coffee hour to connect with one another and welcome new people. I told them that they had become adaptive leaders in working for a solution to their problem.

Then one person asked, "But how are we going to get people to volunteer to set up and clean the china?"

Adaptive leadership can be difficult, and it isn't always intuitive. Adaptive leadership requires us to admit that we can't always identify the real problem. More importantly, we don't know the solution. Admitting those realities makes us feel ineffective and incompetent. It can make those we lead question our skills. Easy answers are the stuff of short committee meetings. Assigning tasks for three committee members makes us look effective. But it will likely yield poor results in the long run.

Adaptive leadership is not easy. In fact, in the short run, adaptive leaders will face serious resistance. Often this comes in the form of sabotage.

Sabotage

Juan was an interim pastor following a pastor who had served the congregation for twenty-eight years. Although things seemed to be going well, under the surface things were boiling. He made several changes in the worship service, and his style was quite different from that of his predecessor. At a session meeting, Juan suggested that the proceeds of an upcoming missional fundraiser go to a ministry that he knew well. The session agreed that this sounded like a good match, and the motion was unanimously approved. A week later, a member of the session approached Juan. She explained that she had been talking with her fellow session members and that they had decided to fund another ministry. Juan later discovered that she had called all the members and persuaded them to change their votes. She was sabotaging his ministry.

When we stretch a rubber band, we feel tension. Every time we pull the band into a different shape, an opposing force naturally results. Likewise, in our churches, when leaders stretch the system into another form, they will feel the opposing force of sabotage. In his book *Failure of Nerve*, Edwin Friedman writes that sabotage often results when we make progress on changing the system.[8] It can come in many forms—blaming, scapegoating, and outright mutiny.

Returning to Chloe

For the first few days after Chloe hit her pandemic breaking point, she slept and read murder mysteries. When she neglected to join a denominational committee meeting on Zoom, her friend Jackie checked in on her. They arranged to meet at a lunch spot with outdoor seating.

It took all the energy Chloe could muster to emerge from her cocoon, but she was relieved when she did. Jackie understood congregational systems well and had the tools to help Chloe understand her context. As Chloe and Jackie talked over tacos, Chloe's context became clear.

Chloe explained that when the pandemic hit, her congregation became more polarized. "We used to have a broad spectrum of beliefs, but we no longer function well together. They're fighting over masks, and the temperature is hot! The mask people think that the no-mask people are threatening their lives. The no-mask people think that the mask people are taking away their freedom. They run to extremes and have lost any ability to compromise."

Jackie dipped her chip into the salsa bowl and nodded. "You're working in a church with a high level of anxiety. When the fear factor was low, they could work with one another. But in a global pandemic, everyone's on high alert. They are in survival mode. They're not only scared about lower attendance and giving; they're worried about their personal mortality. They have lost their flexibility and have become much more reactive. How are you responding in all of this?"

Chloe said, "At first, when the tensions grew and the congregation began to complain more, I could handle it. I listened to the grievances and negotiated compromises, but it didn't work."

"Why?"

"I guess we weren't getting to the real problem. We were trying to sort through data and make policies. But the data constantly changed, and we kept having to come up with new rules. We never got to the root issue—which was the fear and distrust that grew up in all of this."

Jackie nodded, "That makes sense. We all feel better for a little while when we keep the peace. That's the fleeting beauty of technical leadership. Seminaries and churches train us to smooth things over. And since many of us like to avoid conflict, keeping the peace is our default mode. Ultimately, though, you and the church will be healthier if you can pull at the root issues of the conflicts and determine adaptive solutions.

"What finally drove you over the edge?" Jackie asked.

"An elder complained to my personnel committee. She said I wasn't doing enough. I could have handled that. But then the personnel committee took the elder's side, focused on the concerns, and piled on. I felt crushed. The mere thought of doing more broke me." Chloe put down her fork and began to wring her hands.

"Of course, you felt that way," Jackie nodded. "You wanted to fix things—except the solution wasn't for you to do more because the problem wasn't about you. That elder was responding to the anxiety in the church. It's been through the roof for all of us! And you know how people start to sabotage when that fear gets out of control. You need to spend some time celebrating the fact that you got your church through a very difficult situation."

Chloe hadn't recognized the sabotage until Jackie said it. Instead, she had felt the blow as a personal attack. By focusing on the personal aspects of the complaints, she missed an opportunity to see her amazing work. In a very difficult time, she had led her church through change rather than collapse. Her leadership had stretched the congregation, which had resulted in tension and sabotage. That was the system's natural impulse to bring the church back to homeostasis. But eventually Chloe had brought them through it.

At the end of the lunch, Chloe wanted to give Jackie a hug, but they awkwardly settled on the weird elbow bump that had replaced the embrace.

As Chloe drove home, she became amazed at how nice it was to do something for herself. She realized that when the anxiety rose and she had tried to morph into Superpastor, she had sacrificed self-care. That significantly contributed to her downward spiral. During times of stress, self-care needed to become a driving force. But they were the moments when she became the least motivated to care for herself.

Chloe made a promise to herself that she would set aside one afternoon in the week to do something to nourish her body and soul. She thought about going for a hike, going to a park, or reading a book. She always had at least one meeting a week in the evenings, so taking an afternoon off made sense.

Like Chloe, when we have suffered through the blaming, scapegoating, or mutinying of sabotage, we will end up with bruises. As we tend to those sore places, we can begin to understand why and how the larger body has reacted. As we pray for healing, compassion may grow, helping us understand the fear and anxiety that haunt individuals and spread throughout the church. Understanding that fear and how it functions within our congregations will help us to predict and anticipate the response to our actions. Foreseeing the reactions and reminding ourselves that "this is the system" will help us not to take the resistance and sabotage personally. It will also allow us to regulate our emotions when we want to react defensively.

The more we can understand and anticipate how the congregation will respond, the more effective we can be at reducing the overall anxiety in the system. And we will bring ourselves one step closer to healing.

Reflection Prompts

1. *Get distance from the system.* Oftentimes, you will be attacked when the church system is reacting to something that has nothing to do with you. If you have evaluated and weighed the complaints and realize that people are reacting to the system and not something you have done, you need to look into the mirror and say to yourself, "It's not about me." Literally and out loud, you can say, "It's not about me," every day. You may even buy a dry-erase marker and scrawl, "It's not about you," across your mirror. The mantra can be important to differentiate yourself from the stress of the church body.

2. You might also *get distance from the system by going away and gaining perspective.* Consider friends or relatives you can visit. Or go away on vacation. A different context and rhythm for a week can give you perspective on your situation.

3. *Recognize acute anxiety.* What acute anxiety are your parishioners facing? Is there a short-term stressor from which they will recover? Have they faced the loss of an important member? Have they had a recent pastoral transition?

4. *Recognize chronic anxiety.* What chronic anxiety is your church facing? Has there been a decade-long decline in membership? Are church members worried that they will not be able to survive another generation? Was there a trauma, such as a betrayal of pastoral trust, that has lived on through generations? What symptoms does the chronic anxiety produce? For example, does your church have a lack of trust when it comes to money? Do members react strangely to youth group trips? Do members of the congregation seem to hide facts when someone mentions the drinking habits of the former pastor? All of these things might indicate a reactive system—a church with a high level of chronic anxiety that makes all its members prone to reactivity.

5. *Name the homeostasis.* Can you name some obvious dysfunctions in your church body that people refuse to change because it will upset homeostasis? Here are some examples of homeostasis. Do any apply to you? Can you think of others?

- The choir director constantly criticizes the pastor, but the personnel committee and board refuse to do anything about it because it will upset the choir members.
- The head usher is rude to children and parents who come into the sanctuary. She forces parents to take their children into the nursery, even when they don't want to. But no one wants to replace her because she has done the job of recruiting ushers for many years.
- Young families begin coming to church, but the older members don't like the noise that the children make, so they start complaining and giving the parents dirty looks.
- The stewardship committee refuses to give a positive report. Year after year they try to raise funds by stating, "We are on the verge of death! Send us your money!" When you offer more positive messaging, they respond that people won't give unless they know the situation is dire. And so the church is never able to celebrate its abundance.

6. *Face the sabotage.* Are there people in the church who routinely undermine the leadership? Can you name them? Are you able to identify what they fear? Do you have any allies who will stand up for you?

7. *Tell a story about your context.* What are the historic insights that you have gleaned? How does your church typically handle conflict or trauma? Can you share your insights with new leaders so they are aware of the patterns?

Part Two

Healing Our Lives

Chapter Five

Recognizing Our Reactions

When Frederick first started at his position, he met Christine, a prominent lay leader in the congregation. The church had conducted a long and arduous search process before it called Frederick, and Christine had kept the church running during the transitions. He listened closely to her comments, and she had many valuable insights about how the church ought to run. She stood beside him as they worked to get the committees in the church functioning effectively. They got many of the safety procedures the denomination recommended in place, such as making sure that the offering was counted by two people and that two adults were present with the children of the church.

At first, Christine's comments felt constructive. Then when those initial difficulties had been resolved, Christine's keen critical eye focused on Frederick. When Frederick would host an educational event, Christine would wonder why more people weren't there. When he sent out emails informing the congregation of an upcoming event, she complained that he should have called members on the phone instead. Then she began to criticize the content of the events. Each criticism paralyzed Frederick with anxiety.

After a year, Christine's attacks became even more personal, demeaning his character and questioning his integrity. She became hypercritical of his office hours, noting when he left for lunch and when he came back. Confused at how she knew so much about his calendar, Frederick realized that his office manager was reporting his whereabouts to Christine, making him feel doubly under attack.

He sensed his blood pressure rise each time he saw Christine's name on his phone. He felt like a child as he avoided her calls. Every time Christine complained, which seemed constant, he froze.

Frederick felt like he was back at home with his father, who criticized every move that he made. Frederick could never satisfy his father. When his father was dying, Frederick began to sort out and understand his father's narcissistic tendencies. He realized that his father had always treated him as an extension of his own dreams and insecurities, creating expectations to which Frederick could never live up. In Frederick's grief, Christine became another version of Frederick's helicopter dad, who hovered over his childhood. And when he saw her, he transformed into that little boy, frozen in place, terrified of taking a step, because he knew it would be the wrong step.

Frederick didn't freeze intentionally. He would mean to call Christine back, and he would put the call on his to-do list, and then it would stay on that list until he assumed he would talk to her in person. But then he would see her at a church function and dodge her. When he could not elude her, he just listened to a one-sided monologue, never able to respond. Soon he began to do the bare minimum at his job. He stopped bringing up new ideas at all because he knew it would be an invitation for criticism.

Finally, Frederick began to recognize that he was playing an adult version of the children's game red light, green light. Whenever he saw Christine, she was his red light. Frederick needed to identify his reactions so that he could figure out how to get unstuck and maintain a healthier relationship with his church leadership.

Understanding Our Reactions

Frederick became reactive in his relationship with Christine, which impaired his ability to function as a pastor. What is reactivity? Reactivity is the emotional response to the anxiety we feel at that moment. We each have a certain capacity to control our reactivity, but once the anxiety (which we also call stress) reaches a certain level, our emotions take over and we react. What that level is differs for each of us each day. As we learned in the previous chapter, many factors influence our reactivity. For instance, being hungry or tired makes us less able to regulate our emotions. So how do we react when we reach that point? Do we yell and scream? Do we become quiet and refuse to engage? Do we take it out on those around us?

If you aren't sure how you express your reactivity, ask a loved one or two—they will know exactly how you react. We are not at our best during those reactive moments, and we might try to forget them, for good reason. However, we need to examine them. It is important to know how we react because we hope to minimize these moments. As leaders in a very anxious system, we need to avoid being reactive as much as humanly possible.

You may say, "We are human, and reacting emotionally is part of being human!" That is correct. However, to lead effectively in an anxious system, we need to *project* a less anxious presence.[1] Internally we may feel the same anxiety, but if we can outwardly project a less anxious presence, we will help the system to lower its overall anxiety level.

So how do we project a less anxious presence? Before we can work on that, we need to look at a few more dynamics of the church system. We can ask, *How do we operate within the organization? How do other members function? How do we deal with anxiety?* Every system has patterns that play out. The first two are reciprocal patterns of overfunctioning and underfunctioning. The third we will discuss is triangulation, bringing in the dreaded third person.

Overfunctioning

Pastors tend to overfunction in a system. How do you know if this is your go-to reaction? One major warning sign is that you take up the responsibility for making the congregation feel good. When anxiety arises around stewardship, you think it's your job to bring peace to the situation and placate any anger. When fear rears its ugly head around a disaster, you step in heroically and create unity in the congregation. In day-to-day interactions, your skills have been invaluable to the members, as you have been the one to soothe the most contrarian factions within the leadership. You pick up the phone late at night when your most unstable parishioner calls. You drop every-thing, even your much-awaited family vacation, to conduct a funeral, because the congregation needs *you*, their pastor. You are also a suc-cessful pastor because your skills are highly prized in ministry.

When frustration arises, you attempt to fix it by working harder. You have picked up a huge array of knowledge from the pastorate, from plumbing to web design, because you have slipped into the dif-ferent jobs as needed.

Unfortunately, you may have done all this caring without ever thinking about your own needs. You rarely ask for a pay increase, and the denomination must force your church to meet the minimum salary requirements. In fact, you have not gotten any increases in salary, even though the staff has gotten smaller and you have taken up all the additional work. Your parsonage is full of things that the church has not gotten around to fixing. You might have welcomed a huge array of cast-off furniture to your home because someone in your congregation needed to get rid of it.

Long ago you stopped expecting good things from the congrega-tion. Your internal mantra has become, "It's just a lot easier to do this myself." It's not only the small things, like rearranging chairs before a meeting, but you have stopped expecting the big things too. No one thanks you for your sermons or recognizes your work. No one notices important anniversaries, even when you bring them to the church's attention. No one tries to pay you for funerals or weddings, and they don't acknowledge the extra hours they take out of your work week. There are no Christmas cards at the end of the year. People grumble about how much vacation time you get, and they text you on your days off. If you ignore the texts, then they begin to call.

Reciprocity and deference no longer exist. At first you cherished being approachable. Now all the respect has evaporated from the pastoral relationship. After a few years, all of this has begun to wear on you. You might tell yourself that you're a "servant" who "takes up the cross daily." But you're no one's savior. You are vulnerable and you have needs.

Not only that, but as you overfunction, the church becomes less healthy. The members rely on you for everything. It is comforting to be needed so much. It makes you feel valuable. Yet you realize that the church can barely go one Sunday without you there before everything feels like it will fall apart. When it does crumble, the members don't notice how much they rely upon you and respond with gratitude and praise (as you might secretly hope); instead, they get angry. They want you to formalize a massive training program on top of doing everything by yourself. So you put together a weekend event to train people, but when you ask for volunteers, no one steps up to help.

What are some tips for working in an environment that expects you to overfunction? What happens when you have the tendency to work harder in the hope of relieving an anxious church? Often it comes down to keeping boundaries. Knowing where you end and the church begins is key.

Ask yourself what you get by overfunctioning. The sad truth is that as much as you might complain about overfunctioning, you get something from it. You might validate yourself and help soothe your insecurities. If you love to hear people say, "You need to take a break! You do so much!" then you might need to be needed. Yet as you recognize that this isn't healthy for you, you'll have to do some digging around in your own history to figure out why you get so much affirmation from overfunctioning.

Help empower laypeople. Ask yourself, "What tasks am I completing that church members should be doing themselves?" Keep a list, and assign the tasks to committees and individuals. This process takes a long time. It takes a while to know what gifts and abilities church members have. People will push back against healthier systems. It won't be easy, but keep working on the list.

Evaluate tech boundaries. Are there ways in which you can make your tech boundaries more secure so that you can maintain privacy and be sure that you're not on call every moment of the day and night? Make sure that you have a healthy relationship with your parishioners on social media. They don't need to know what you're up to and thinking at every moment of the day. Also, the members of your church should not expect you to respond to them at all hours. You can turn off notifications on your phone so you can rest. You can keep your work and personal email separate. Carefully note which form of communication feels most invasive, and be clear about what you need. Do you prefer texts or phone calls? Do you work in your office and appreciate people calling you on your office phone? Or would you rather work from other locations and have them call you on your cell phone?

Protect your time off. Do you use all your time off? Do you have adequate coverage during vacations if there is an emergency? You might want to have friends or family members keep you accountable for making sure that you don't spend your Sabbath answering email.

Underfunctioning

On the flip side, you might underfunction, allowing members of the congregation (sometimes a couple of bullies) to take over the leadership of the church. Roger began his time at First Presbyterian excited about ministry. He had always been passionate about antiracism, and he was called to a white congregation in an evolving neighborhood. As more immigrants moved into the community, the church wanted to reach out to its new neighbors, and Roger seemed the perfect person to help them with their new mission.

Roger was bursting with ideas, but when he began to share them with the congregation, he realized that they could never get off the ground. The projects always stalled due to a variety of reasons, like budget constraints or insurance liabilities. The congregation always needed more information before they could step out; they needed more data. Then when Roger would come up with all the data that supported the idea, they would complain that the project didn't solve the "real" problems, making the perfect the enemy of the good.

As Roger started to work with the congregation more, he noticed that two couples ran every committee. He thought that the nominating committee must have had the pair on speed dial, but then he realized that they chaired the nominating committee too. They made every decision and sidelined any member or pastor who didn't agree with them. They hardly thought to ask for Roger's guidance before the deed was already done. He found out about meetings after they occurred and employees after they had been hired.

Soon, Roger realized that no one shared his vision or respected his leadership. His successes in former congregations were seen as geographic oddities, things that would only happen "in the Bible belt." He tried to fight for his ideas, but then he became embarrassed by the constant rejection. He had always been a rising star in the denomination, but now he felt like he wasn't a strong enough leader. He wondered what was wrong with him. He started to dread any new idea that popped up in his mind, because he knew that it would end up as another failure.

Roger began to take the path of least resistance; after all, he didn't go into the ministry to constantly argue over line items and insurance liabilities. Plus, he found that the less he cared, the more people seemed to like him. So he became less engaged and allowed the power-hungry couple to get their way, even when he knew it would be devastating for the church. Roger slept later and went into the office for shorter amounts of time. With all the autonomy and creativity taken from his position, Roger felt the joy drain away. Depression crept in, and it felt like the church had sucked out the last bit of energy that Roger had to offer the world. He couldn't think of anything to look forward to, other than retirement, so he dreamed about retirement all the time.

A few members of the church complained about his complacency, and they wondered what had happened to all his passion. The membership got smaller each year, but the church was much more comfortable without Roger's energy getting in the way of their life together.

Meanwhile, Roger's depression began to affect his health. The air got heavier, and peeling himself out of the covers became a chore for Roger. If a sickness lingered anywhere in the vicinity, then Roger would certainly catch it. He got every flu, virus, and stomach ailment. When the pandemic hit, Roger began to work remotely. That gave him the opportunity to work in his pajamas, take afternoon naps, and eventually spend most of the day chilling in front of the television.

At first, his partner felt relieved after so many years of watching Roger work tirelessly, but Roger's inactivity grew alarming as his depression increased. Then the warning bells grew loud and clear when Roger began drinking during work hours.

Roger underfunctioned in his congregation. If this is your tendency, then you might respond to the continued resistance in your congregation by giving up. Often churches can be places where great ideas go to die, and if you're creative at heart, then congregational ministry could become a dreadful place. An overfunctioning system might be full of people who are power hungry and controlling. If your vision and leadership ideas become constantly locked in a battle of wills, then you might find that it's easier to put your energy someplace else.

How do you fight lethargy when the church system works to weaken your leadership?

Evaluate your mental health. If you feel depressed, then a professional needs to assess what's happening. Some pastors go through situational depression, where external forces cause the mental health issue. During the pandemic, many ministers slipped into this state. But other church leaders have depression that is more organic, and they might switch from job to job, call to call, trying to find a place that will make them happy. Then they realize that they are trying to find an external solution for an internal problem. They might need a steady schedule of therapy, exercise, and/or medication instead of a new job.

Keep moving forward. It is easy to stop functioning when you face resistance, but any time you move forward you will face headwinds. Remember that many organizations (and especially churches) evolve to arrest any sort of development. The easiest way for an organization to resist change is to undermine effective leadership. If members stop your leadership on a regular basis, do what you can to keep the progress happening. Try not to allow motions to be tabled indefinitely. Keep bringing difficult items to the table, even when one person on the board opposes them. Do not allow bullies to hold ministry hostage.

Keep social connections. Do you isolate? Do you resist leaving your house and avoid social interactions? Are you relying more on delivery services that leave food and items on your front porch? Often lethargy turns into isolation, and it can become a precursor to addiction. Watch for the ways that you isolate and work to maintain connections.

Hold on to a mantra or metaphor. Pray and open yourself to a symbol, saying, or Scripture passage that you can repeat to yourself. Clichés might be annoying when other people say them to you, but they can be great when they bubble up from your own experience—for example, "Everyone likes progress, but no one likes change." You might also want to repeat a Scripture verse—for example, "Without vision, the people will perish" (Proverbs 29:18 KJV). Or there might be a metaphor that sustains you. When you feel like giving up, you may think about a large rock that will withstand any storm.

Be aware of your energy. If you feel yourself beginning to underfunction, see if you can find a creative outlet adjacent to church work. For instance, is there a digital ministry that you could expand? Or is there a nonprofit in the area that you could work with? Is there an arts program (writing or visual) where you could focus your energy? Would this be a good time to pursue some continuing education? If the system doesn't allow for your energy and growth, you can find other ways to tend to it.

Roger began to figure a way out of his underfunctioning after a friend drove him to a 12-step meeting. He realized that his isolation had led to his drinking too much and that he had become an alcoholic. Through the program, he made friends and maintained deep connections with other people.

Slowly he learned to do other things to fight the lethargy. Roger reported that keeping a strict routine became vital as he learned to function in a healthy manner. He began the day with prayer and reading a spiritual book. He ate proper meals. After the pandemic, his church relaxed office hours so that Roger could telecommute, but he knew that this would not be healthy for him. So he persisted in keeping office hours even when he didn't have to.

Roger also learned that he vacillated from overfunctioning to underfunctioning. Often when he overfunctioned for a long time, he would cope by underfunctioning, so he learned to be aware of his boundaries. When he became clear about his office hours and times when he would respond to communication, the church did not respond well. But eventually he was able to maintain a healthier relationship with the members.

Triangulation

Triangulation is another way that we react to anxiety in a system. Although we spend most of our lives in one-on-one relationships, we also spend a great deal of time talking to others about those relationships (some of us more than others). This is because, according to Bowen, two-person relationships are unstable. He writes, "The triangle is the basic molecule of an emotional system. It is the smallest stable relationship unit."[2] By "stable relationship" Bowen does not mean "better relationship." "Stable" here refers to less anxiety. Some forms of triangulation are healthy and normal; after all, a three-legged stool is more stable than a two-legged one. When tension arises between two people, a third person is often needed to help solve problems and release the anxiety. We rely on friends, therapists, moderators, or others who reside outside of our immediate situation.

The primary purpose of triangulation is to reduce our anxiety and help us feel better. You have a fight with your spouse, and you call a friend. You tell your friend what your spouse did, and the friend responds, "Your spouse is so awful." And you feel better. Your friend confirms that it is all your spouse's fault. You lower your anxiety, but you do nothing to repair the relationship. This is the problem with triangulation. Rather than repairing relationships, triangulation helps us to do nothing, and the damage grows. Ultimately, a good friend would encourage you to talk through the problem with your spouse. But that would probably make you less likely to call that friend because that would not be reducing the anxiety but heightening it.

In the church this happens all the time. One parishioner calls another about problems with the pastor. How often have you heard about a parishioner who is unhappy with you without ever hearing from the person directly? Toxic triangles work extraordinarily well in congregations. The tendency to coat everything with a veneer of niceness makes it so that people don't communicate directly with one another. The minister is usually an outsider, trying to fit in like the new kid at middle school, while the parishioner has decades of history and relationships with other members. Sometimes the parishioner has been the backbone of the community, while the pastor is just trying to learn everyone's names.

In each triangle there are three positions. The following example illustrates each of these positions:

- Alex and Becca are a couple, and Claire is Becca's friend.
- Alex and Becca have a fight.
- Becca calls Claire.

At the beginning, Alex and Becca's anxiety level is very high and Claire's is low. Becca tells Claire about how awful Alex is and about all the mean things he said last night. In this conversation, Becca shifts some of her anxiety to Claire, resulting in Becca's anxiety lowering and Claire's rising. Alex's anxiety remains high, but as he experiences Becca with lower anxiety, he feels even more anxious; importantly, he also feels like an outsider in this triangle and more distant from his wife, who has pushed him to the outside of the triangle.

Note that this example doesn't have any details. What were Alex and Becca arguing about? Does it matter? No, because understanding how the triangle operates is much more important than the topic being communicated. We can get caught up with the content when ultimately it is the communication pattern that is the most damaging to relationships. Therapists are trained to ignore the content and identify the patterns. Likewise, we can map our own triangles to identify our patterns.

Mapping Out the Triangles

One way to gain a better understanding of conflict in a church system is to map out the triangles as you discover them. You can do this in a private journal, and it can be as simple as three names with lines connecting them. You may be tempted to add the content of the conversations, but that is counterproductive. The purpose of this exercise is to help you see who is connected to whom and ultimately with whom you will need to talk to try and deflate the triangles.

We will begin with a common triangle: the senior pastor, the associate pastor, and a parishioner. If you have ever served as an associate pastor or in any staff position in a church, you will have many examples of this triangle. It looks like this:

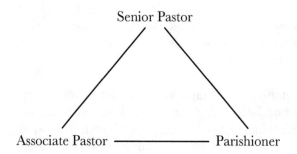

In this example the senior pastor is in the outside position. The parishioner complains about the senior pastor to the associate pastor. What's the complaint? Again, it doesn't matter. You know the complaints. The dynamic of this relationship has the potential of damaging the ministry of the church, and many senior pastors have experienced the problems with this triangle.

This simple triangle can do a great deal of damage. But in a significant conflict, we rarely see only one simple triangle. When we map the relationships, we realize that interlocking triangles exist. An interlocking triangle is a simple triangle connected to another triangle or triangles. These multiple triangles are needed when the anxiety level is high. Remember that the purpose of the triangle is to reduce the anxiety of the person who initiates the triangle. When the anxiety is high, multiple people need to be triangled to reduce the person's anxiety sufficiently. As that anxiety is shifted to others, they need to triangle to reduce their own anxiety.

To return to our simple senior pastor–associate pastor–parishioner triangle, we learn that a parishioner has been in contact with a retired pastor who served this congregation previously. And the retired pastor has complained to the district superintendent. The map now looks like this:

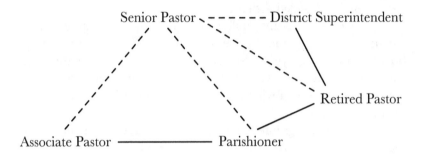

As you can see, the map gets far more complicated as we portray these relationship triangles. Anxiety flows from one person to another, and although these triangles can help reduce the anxiety for some, for those on the outside of the triangle the anxiety only grows. The dotted lines indicate individuals who are not directly in communication with each other. This also makes it clear that the senior pastor is on the outside of all of these triangles. That might seem extreme, but it is experienced by far too many pastors. We have been isolated and pushed to the outside by staff, parishioners, colleagues, and supervisors. So what do we do if we find ourselves in this position? We need to project a less anxious presence.

How to Be a Less Anxious Presence

We know what you're thinking: "Are you nuts? I'm being attacked, I'm isolated, and I need to be less anxious? How?" We both have been in this position and know how hard it is to project a less anxious presence.[3]

When you are in the moment, you have the powerful tool of your breath.[4] A lot of things happen in your body when someone yells at you during a congregational meeting or when you read an ALL CAPS EMAIL!!! As you experience a stressful situation, you respond with a flood of hormones that make your heart beat faster and your blood pressure rise. The anxiety releases blood sugar and fats into your bloodstream. You also begin to breathe more rapidly. The extra oxygen in your brain makes you more alert. You might feel like an old car engine, flooded with gas.

We have the amazing ability to regulate our own physiology, through breathing, moving, and touching.[5] Taking seven deep breaths can change your body chemistry and counteract the fear. You can breathe deeply, without anyone else even noticing what you're doing. But you will probably be able to feel the response as your body settles.

Another tool for grounding yourself is to focus on your surroundings and engage the five senses. Can you identify

- five things that you see,
- four things that you hear,
- three things that you feel,
- two things that you smell, and
- one thing that you taste?[6]

Meditation and stretching can also connect us with our breath and body. Many pastors find that yoga is particularly helpful in regulating our responses. Online yoga instruction has the advantage of accessibility, although we might miss out on the ways that our brains attune to others in a peaceful setting.[7]

When you're not in the heat of the moment, you can work on long-term strategies. We have learned from our experiences that reducing anxiety comes from deflecting blame, attending to our workload, flattening triangles through more open one-on-one communication, and building support.

Remind yourself that this isn't personal. You are a scapegoat for the system. Because you're the leader, the actors will pile the blame onto you. Focus on the system and your role in it, and notice how others' anxiety shifts to you. When your emotions want you to hide in your bed under the covers until this all goes away, fight that urge. When your sermons have been criticized as meaningless, don't believe it. When you are chastised for not visiting enough, hear it for what it is:

anxiety. Defensiveness only adds anxiety to anxiety. Think in terms of the system and the fear driving the emotions.

If you overfunction or underfunction, work on curbing your tendencies. Pastors commonly overfunction or underfunction in relationship to the church's anxiety. If you find yourself using these reactions, then delegate tasks or step up to leadership. Trying to reduce anxiety with unhealthy functioning will only cause more problems in the system in the future.

Work on the triangles. Map the triangles, and try to get an understanding of where the anxiety exists and where it spreads. The hard work will be the conversations that you need to have with those connected to you by dotted lines—the people who talk about you instead of to you. They are very happy lowering their anxiety by creating that triangle. Confronting them needs to be done in a pastoral and caring way. Remember that they are part of the system that is generating the anxiety, and although they may blame you, they are not your enemy. They are pawns of the system. Hear their concerns, treat them with kindness, and do not be defensive or reactive. These may be some of the most difficult conversations you will have as a pastor, but you can manage them.

Finally (although this is not the last thing that you do but the first), *build support both inside and outside of the church.* You need support networks that allow you to process the difficult work you are doing. This is so important for the success of your ministry that we covered it early in this book, and we will continue to return to it. In the development of these support systems, especially the ones inside of the church, be sure not to let the situation become "us against them."[8] When we start to define those voicing concerns as "them," we are setting up a dynamic of sides that makes it hard to recognize that we are all working for the best of the same congregation. Try to stay curious and to maintain connections.

Returning to Frederick

As time went by, Frederick worked hard at reacting less to the anxiety in the church, and this helped. He learned to push through his urge to give up and underfunction. He found increasing support from members of the governing board as they began to realize the impact of Christine's criticisms and stalling tactics. The backing was helpful, and everything seemed to be moving again.

At the new year, however, a number of the supportive governing board members rotated off and new members were elected. At the very first meeting, Christine criticized the board's past decisions and secured enough votes to stall Frederick's initiatives again. Frederick began working on his resume. He was done. This was it. He could not imagine going through another year of stalling. His anxiety level was way too high.

Christine's actions were frustrating and irritating, but did they warrant the level of reactivity from Frederick that they received? Here is a general rule: Whenever a situation generates a higher emotional reaction than it should, something else is at play. It was frustrating that the governing board seemed to return to its previous, less helpful state, but that wasn't a reason for Frederick to leave. All the unresolved wounds and scars from Frederick's relationship with his father and Christine's earlier antics fueled that strong emotional response.

We often carry the pain of the past into the relationships of the present. When we see this happening, we need to reflect on the accomplishments we have made and put things into perspective. Even if we do all the work to get our reactivity to a healthy level, it only takes one emotional landmine to trigger us and let our emotions dominate. We can't let emotion dominate our rationality. It's good to be a person with emotions, but it is less helpful to let our emotions overpower our rational decision-making process.

With the help of friends, a therapist, and board members, Frederick gained a healthy perspective on his context and what activated his response. With his therapist, he named his emotions and found appropriate places to release his turmoil of anger and fear so that they didn't control his decision-making process. He began running, which gave him a physical release, a connection with nature, and time to process. Frederick also spent a lot of time with friends. With them, he sometimes talked about the church. Other times, he got some relief from the drama through playing pickleball. With board members, he learned to rely on those who were supportive of moving forward in their ministry together.

Once we have a chance to diagnose the wound—to look at it, see the context, and understand our reactions—we will be able to tend to it with more knowledge. In the healing process, we can begin by setting boundaries.

Reflection Prompts

1. *Work with your body.* So many of our reactions reside in our bodies. They are primal, and we may not even know how we react, just as we don't understand why our lower leg jumps up when we are hit in the knee at a particular spot. If you feel comfortable, you can explore the ways that you respond to anxiety or stress with movement.

   - Imagine a moment of conflict in your church or childhood. Now get into a fighting posture. You might want to be a wrestler who is getting ready to make his next move. You might want to get your claws out like a mama bear. How did the reaction feel to you? Did it make sense to you?
   - Conjure up the conflict again. Now think about running away. If you have the space to run, then do it. How did fleeing feel for you? Was that a comfortable reaction?
   - Go back to the conflict once again in your mind. Freeze. How does freezing feel?

2. *Journal about your reactions.* Did one of your reactions make more sense in your body than the others? If so, why?

3. *Find correlations.* Is there a correlation between how you react in your body and how you react at your job? For instance, if you feel most comfortable in the fighting position, do you find yourself arguing over petty things? If running away comes naturally, do you often have the urge to quit? If you freeze, do you have the tendency to underfunction?

4. *Map your triangles.* When you map the hot triangles in your congregation, is there a way to flatten any of them? If you find that you are the outsider in the threesome, can you talk directly to someone in the triangle?

5. *Engage in breath prayer.* You can grasp onto a simple mantra as you breathe in the moment. For example: *Breathing in love. Breathing out fear.* Or you can try other prayers, like this one:

A Prayer
(with Seven Deep Breaths)

Loving God,

1

We breathe in your life,
knowing that in our stories of creation
your breath is our breath.
We breathe out our anxiety,
acknowledging the stress that increases
with every blaring email and dire prediction.

2

We breathe in your hope,
knowing that you can make a way
out of no way.
We breathe out the despondency
that creeps up on us,
paralyzing us from doing good.

3

We breathe in your grace
as we pray for patience with our loved ones
and endurance in this body.
We breathe out our petty annoyances
and menial irritations
that make us forget the importance of our bonds.

4

We breathe in your peace,
which surpasses all our understanding
and guards our hearts and minds.
We breathe out our worries,
all of our need to be in control,
and the tension in our guts.

5

We breathe in your abundance,
knowing that we have enough
when we live as a beloved community.
We breathe out our fear of scarcity
that whispers lies to us
and keeps our fists clenched in greed.

6

We breathe in your wisdom
that keeps perspective in our crisis,
reminding us of what is important.
We breathe out despair
that blocks us from seeing possibilities
and blinds us from your vision.

7

We breathe in your love,
knowing that your presence surrounds us
and encircles us.
We breathe out our suffering,
acknowledging that our pain happens
within your loving embrace.

Chapter Six

Setting Our Boundaries

When Sarah had an affair with an elder in her congregation, it didn't make any sense. He did not attract her or charm her. In fact, his infuriatingly sexist politics repulsed her. That one night certainly did not warrant the eventual outcome—the destruction of her marriage and career. "I was just so tired," Sarah confided to a friend over dinner. "I don't know how else to explain it."

Exhaustion and burnout often accompany sexual misconduct—which might confuse us. If a person feels drained, how do they have the energy to engage in an inappropriate relationship? Doesn't sneaking, hiding, and lying take a lot of stamina? Who has time for all that? The answer to that mystery has to do with anxiety and its impact on our boundaries.

Often when ministers take boundary training, it consists of "what not to do" lists: Don't be alone in a room with someone you might be attracted to. Don't communicate in inappropriate ways. And most importantly, don't touch that person in ways that might be construed as intimate.

While the lists are vital, they don't always get to the heart of the matter. Most of us know how to enumerate what not to do. So why do ministers still end up in inappropriate relationships? In our boundary training, we think about what the church needs, but we don't always think about what *we* need. We don't learn how to keep boundaries around ourselves for the purpose of protecting *our* expectations, relationships, beliefs, and identities. When we go looking for love in all the wrong places, our training can address the "how" issues without wrestling with the deeper "why" question: *Why do we wander for affection?* Proper boundaries allow us to have the space and ability to explore that question, they allow us to differentiate from the church, and they allow us to care for ourselves.

If we violate boundaries, it is almost always due to a perfect storm of conditions. It begins when our stress levels are extremely high. This high level of anxiety will exacerbate our feelings of being wounded, exhausted, and burned-out, so we need something to help us feel better. Our need to find relief from the anxiety will lead us to triangulating and sometimes lowering or ignoring our boundaries. And of course, all this can lead to a life-altering experience that can even leave us wondering, "What did I do?"

Boundaries are important, but not just because of the physical time-out they can bring to a sexually charged relationship. They also give us the space to detangle ourselves from the anxiety that makes us feel so tired in the first place. In that space with well-established boundaries, we can process the damage and differentiate in an intensely emotional context. We can get to a place where we can ask ourselves, "Are we depleted? Have we neglected to take care of our core needs? Has our ego been damaged? Do we need healing?"

Boundaries and Self-Differentiation

As you think about boundaries, imagine poaching an egg. To poach an egg, you boil a pot of water and use a spoon to whirl the water. Then you crack the egg into the boiling water. The white of the egg has a different consistency than the yolk and will swirl around a bit in the bubbling liquid, sometimes making strings. The art of poaching an egg lies in making sure that the yolk remains soft and runny while also remaining in its membrane. A delicious poached egg will have a yolk that won't break *or* become too hard.

Imagine that the mini tornado of boiling water represents your congregation, and the egg stands in for you. The yolk is your core self. The white is your pseudo self.[1] Your core self is the authentic person you are. It shines when you feel secure. It appears when you don't have to be on guard for a four-letter word slipping out of your mouth. It arrives when you can speak freely about your political views without worrying about judgment, drama, or a church split. Your core self can admit to unpopular opinions. It can step out of the closet and refuse to star in awkward gender roles. It doesn't feel responsible for entertaining everyone or controlling their emotions. It shows sincere affection, tenderness, and vulnerability.

Your pseudo self includes the masks you wear so that people will like you or so that you will be professionally acceptable. It includes the words you use and the opinions you espouse to be accepted and fit in with those around you. The pseudo self is not necessarily a bad thing. It's simply the suit you put on to preach when you'd rather wear sweatpants. It's the smile you greet your congregation with, even though moments earlier you yelled at your kids to get them out the door. The pseudo self knows how to code-switch and adapt. Your pseudo self also includes your supersize reactions and all your defense mechanisms.

In our metaphor, when you maintain good boundaries, the white of the egg remains in one piece and the yolk stays whole. In family systems parlance, this goes back to the concept of differentiation, which we covered in chapter 3. You want to remain in the boiling water and stay connected without losing shape and definition. This process is more of an art than any list of rules indicates.

Lost Boundaries

Now imagine poaching several eggs at the same time. If you've done this, you know what it looks like. Egg whites get everywhere, connecting all the eggs together in a fused mess. In the same way, we can fuse with other people. We become fused with the emotions of the congregation, feeding off their anxiety and fear. This phenomenon is called herding.[2] Anxiety in the church system is tamed by a false harmony as pseudo selves take control and dominate the rational approach. We see this all the time in the church, when one antagonist has a problem with a proposed plan by the governing board and everyone bends to that one person's discomfort and delays the process. Congregations avoid conflicts at all costs, leaving the most anxious person controlling the outcome. Even if we try to speak up, members rarely hear us over the deafening static of anxiety in the system.

What does it look like when pastors do not differentiate themselves from their congregations? Here are a few examples.

- *Addicted to adoration.* A pastor cannot bear to live without the compliments at the end of every service or a generous Christmas bonus.
- *Crushed by criticism.* A pastor ruminates on the smallest complaint, even if it's from someone who hasn't been to church in a year. Her ears are tuned in to any slight. She becomes a people pleaser, to the point where she questions her own leadership at every step.
- *Overcomplying to expectations.* A pastor finds out that his predecessor only took one week of vacation, even though the contract includes four. The church expects the current pastor to abide by the previous pastor's bad standard, and he doesn't have the resolve to stand up for himself or fight it, so he bends to the church's expectation.
- *Preaching preferences become priority.* Someone in the congregation tells the pastor how he should preach, and he conforms—even when he ends up espousing a theology that he doesn't believe. For instance, a member tells Rev. George that the church doesn't talk about politics, and "politics" means everything from providing meals for people without homes, to being antiracist, to caring for God's creation. George goes along with this, even though he doesn't believe that he should.
- *Assuming anxiety.* Members become anxious about attendance and income, and the pastor begins to adopt their fears. She tries to manage the church's emotional state, and it takes a toll. She endures sleepless nights, suffers upset stomachs, or develops an addiction.
- *Identity issues.* Another sign of unhealthy fusion is when pastors have no identity outside of their calling. We rarely have a chance to step away from our role as pastors. Yet we need to find a healthy release and a space in which we can feel fully human.

Unfortunately, the metaphors that we use to describe ministry can also feed into an unhealthy identity. We talk about serving and sacrificing. If you're from a Roman Catholic tradition or you're an LGBTQ pastor serving in a nonaffirming congregation, you may practice celibacy, and you may have been taught that you are married to the church. These might be important correctives for power-hungry, narcissistic pastors, but for most of us they're not. In the midst of the countless "servant leadership" lessons we might have sat through, we have to remember to maintain a healthy sense of self.

The church will take as much as you give. If you sacrifice your all for them, you may have nothing left other than bitterness and resentment.

It's not supposed to be that way. Jesus came so that we might have abundant lives. Your life matters. Your needs matter. Your expectations, beliefs, relationships, and identities all matter—especially when you're a pastor.

Rigid Boundaries

On the other extreme, our boundaries can be too rigid. Pastors can cut themselves off from their congregations, no longer staying in healthy connection with them. They can withdraw and build impenetrable walls around themselves. Pastors often tell each other, "You've got to grow thicker skin!" That might be true (depending on the person), but there is the danger of our skin growing so thick that we stop feeling. How do we know when we have lost connection with the congregation?

- *Emotional impassivity.* Your skin becomes so thick that you lose empathy and compassion. If the patriarch of the church dies during your day off, you refuse to call the family. You can no longer feel the joys or sorrows of ministry.
- *Cutting communication.* The number of unread emails in your inbox hits four digits, and it's not from spam. It's from your utter inability to communicate any longer. You explain to your congregation that you don't like email, but when they try to call or text, you don't respond to those methods either.

Church members realize that they can no longer contact you, and they feed all requests through your office manager or your spouse.

- *Leaving the building.* When you hear the voice of someone in the building, you figure out an exit plan. One pastor who was burned-out in a high-conflict church said he would duck into the sanctuary to "pray" each time a parishioner would enter.
- *Blocking and unfriending.* Maintaining healthy social media boundaries can be important. But if we are cutting people off emotionally, we might block or "unfriend" parishioners in a hurtful manner.
- *Crushing conflict.* If a parishioner disagrees with an idea, you bar that person from all leadership positions. If someone offers constructive criticism, you avoid ever speaking to them again.

Healthy Boundaries

Somewhere between bleeding overcompliance and hardened withdrawal, we can maintain healthy boundaries. They give us the ability to remain emotionally connected to our whirling congregation while maintaining a solid sense of self. You listen to critique while weighing the source and context. You feel pain when you've hurt someone or when someone wounds you. When someone praises you, you don't construct your whole self-esteem around the compliment. Rather, you accept it with gratitude and keep working. When someone criticizes you, you don't let the comment have undue influence. Instead, you consider the source and what that person might be going through. You recognize and acknowledge the tension in the room while imagining yourself rising above it.

How do we keep healthy boundaries?

We begin by realizing that we deserve them. As pastors, our core identity flows from being a beloved child of God, but it's easy to lose sight of that. If you're a woman, a person of color, or an LGBTQ person and feel lucky that you even have a job, then you might need this reminder: You are fully called. God loves you and wants you to have an abundant life (even apart from your vocation).

Jesus' words are golden—you must love your neighbors as you love yourself. But many ministers need to flip the command—you need to love yourself as you love your neighbors. Serving as a pastor often means that you give much more love than you receive. As a result, your reserves dry up and you become weary trying to pump water from an empty well. Your sense of self erodes, and you can become unhealthy. You can forget that you are God's beloved. You don't know why your work matters, and you might even wonder why *you* matter. Then you start looking toward outside sources to convey your worth.

How we find validation can differ. You might begin to rely on church data as a measurable indicator of your value. Your identity becomes tied to the number of people in the pews or the pile in the offering plate. As anxiety in denominations increases, various survey tools will keep emerging to present data in different ways. Surveys might measure the satisfaction of people in your congregation. Denominational leaders love these tools because they feel that in using them they are doing something important, and it gives them a sense of control.

You might begin to lean heavily on the adoration of your congregation as an ego boost. When pastors are looking for that external validation, they can slip into inappropriate relationships with parishioners with the hope that the excitement will revive their parched souls.

Anxiety can dominate our behavior and lead us to destructive actions, or we can set boundaries to protect our precious selves. The boundaries go beyond that list of what not to do. They should completely reorient our lives toward abundant life and God's love. They should encourage us to set parameters on our *expectations, beliefs, relationships, and core identities.*

We often spend our time thinking about what the church needs. In this chapter, as you remind yourself that you are important, we invite you to think about and clearly state what you need. This is different for every person and different from what the church's previous pastor needed. These examples are not meant to be strict mandates, but they are meant to affirm you, if you feel unsteady about asking for what you need.

Expectations

Churches often have obvious unhealthy expectations that we can place boundaries around. Those boundaries often have to do with time, potential, and passions.

The expectation that pastors are to be on call twenty-four hours a day, every day, is not sustainable. Plus, we need to model good spiritual practices for our workaholic culture. We can refuse to answer the phone on our days off. We can check voicemail after a call to find out if it's about the death of a church matriarch or a complaint about too many carnations in the floral arrangements, and then we can respond accordingly. We can word our email's "out of office" response so that people understand that we need our Sabbath. After all, keeping a Sabbath is not only a commandment, but it also allows us to do meaningful ministry and protects us from burning out.

Then we take our other time off, making sure that we have a chance to restore ourselves with vacations, study leave, and sick days. The church can and will run without us being there. If you get sick, take all the uninterrupted time you need. This necessary and regular separation not only allows us to differentiate ourselves from our congregations, but it also keeps us from falling into other unhealthy expectations—such as the savior-complex trap.

The savior-complex trap comes from internal expectations, which are harder to detect. For example, Victor began working in a tiny congregation and soon found out that he was their "make it or break it" pastor. The church had been declining in membership for over fifty years. In their desperation, the members had tried to re-create the church of their past while rejecting the input of the younger generations in their church. The younger members, who didn't live with the same societal expectations to attend church as previous generations, quit going. So as the older generations passed away, the church kept getting smaller. When Victor became their pastor, they pinned all of their hopes and dreams onto him, without changing any of their behaviors. "He is young! He will save us!" Victor almost believed them.

We can easily fall into the savior-complex trap. When people in a church sense that we have the powers to resuscitate their lifeless, near-death bodies, we can allow their magical thinking to define us. Imagining that we could potentially revive a church single-handedly entices us, and there is a whole market of church-growth books suggesting that if we're creative, calculated, and charismatic enough, we can do it. And to have a congregation that thinks revitalization is possible because of *us* is a great ego inflator. It's almost like being the protagonist in a preteen book. The young boy is a loser in one world, but when he moves into an alternative universe, he's the hero that everyone has been looking for! The congregation's unrealistic expectation stealthily becomes our own.

Unfortunately, the reality of the situation settles in quickly. We soon figure out that we don't have that special cult-leader charisma, that we can't save the church with our sheer determination, and that trying to do so will burn us out completely.

There are other expectations that we need to protect. Once, I (Carol) applied for a pastoral position and was told by the search committee that I published too much. I felt called to this church, and the committee's reaction surprised me because I thought that a search committee would see my writing as a good thing, like someone who earned a D.Min. I explained that I wrote on my time off, but the committee remained unconvinced. They asked me to stop writing and assumed that I would be a bad pastor because of my outside interests. They could not see that the practice of writing was making me a healthier human, which in turn made me a better pastor. The rejection made me understand something important: I needed to keep boundaries around my creativity. I could not go to a church that saw my outside interests as a threat to my ministry.

We all need to keep boundaries around the callings and passions that seemingly have nothing to do with the church. Although our jobs are one vocation, we also need to protect our creative pursuits and the things that give us joy.

Beliefs

Another important way that we protect our core sense of self has to do with our beliefs and integrity. On one hand, in this cultural moment of political purity and ostentatious oversharing, pastors often expect one another to be "prophetic," which can mean loudly proclaiming exactly what we think without any sensitivity to the beliefs of those around us. On the other hand, we might be in churches that bully us into professing things that we do not believe. For many denominations, the clergy skew much more liberal than their congregations.[3] As older people have consumed more content from Fox News, the network has become a stronger influence on their beliefs than their pastors or their churches.[4] However, we need to have integrity, to hold on to our beliefs firmly, while staying connected to those who don't agree with us.

When someone does not have a strong sense of their own beliefs, they might go along with the denomination's proclamations, no matter what they might be. We watched this play out for decades as different denominations struggled with rights for LGBTQ people. A pastor might not be able to stand up against bigoted beliefs in the denominational structure because her ethical core has disintegrated into a morass of careerism. She has set aside her conscience in order to vie for a better position. Or her core has turned into a moral chameleon as she has bent to the notions of the largest giver in the church instead of holding fast to what she knows is right.

Our core beliefs are the things we know to be true and do not need to be reinforced or validated by others. Part of the work we each need to do is to gain a better understanding of what we believe. Knowing the core beliefs helps us as we maintain our own belief boundaries. With good humor, we can stay in contact with people who have different opinions. We can have a core sense of belief. We can appreciate the influence of others without caving to it or controlling what others believe.

Relationships

When Mike Pence became a vice presidential candidate, he introduced the nation to the "Billy Graham rule." Pence was added to the ticket to make Donald Trump, the famously philandering presidential candidate, more acceptable to evangelicals. While Trump paid off a porn star and bragged about leering in teenage girls' dressing rooms while they changed, Pence lived by the renowned evangelist

Billy Graham's rule that he would not allow himself to be alone in a room with a woman—aside from his wife or daughters—in case temptation might arise.

Graham created the restriction so that he would remain above reproach. The problem is that the rule, both at church and at business lunches in the political realm, effectively cuts women out of important conversations and decisions. It makes women two-dimensional. Instead of seeing women as multifaceted humans with gifts and abilities to add to a professional conversation, it distills all women into sexual objects, just as quickly as our minds tend to morph that porn star into a two-dimensional caricature. Plus, the restriction doesn't acknowledge the sexual dynamics that can arise between people of the same gender.

The controversy brought up an important conversation about where our boundaries should be, and the danger of responding with immovable concrete walls. Avoiding temptation or scandal is important, but it often requires more work than simply decreasing one's proximity to a potential sex partner. There are deeper questions that we need to ask ourselves as we think about boundaries and relationships. Are we forming our core identity from the adoration of members of the congregation? Have certain church members become an extension of who we are in unhealthy ways?

Maintaining professional boundaries as a pastor can be difficult and confusing, as our relational lines blur. A therapist who sees a client in the grocery store does not talk with him. But it's different for a pastor running into church members. We are part of one another's lives in significant ways that cannot be turned off the moment we leave a service. As pastors, we are even expected to invite ourselves to visit people in their homes when they are most vulnerable.

What sort of boundaries do you need around your relationships? Most of us have some sort of consistent boundary training, which usually centers around protecting church members and assumes that we will be the transgressors. But that's not always the case. It's also good to think about your needs. Do members of the church sexually harass you? If you're single, how will you handle dating? What do you need from the church when it comes to your relationships? If you're going through a divorce, how much do you want the church to know about your private life? What do you want to share about your children? What do you need to keep private about your family? What's appropriate for you when it comes to pastoral care or home visits? What expectations do you need when it comes to your relationships? Often we bow to the expectations and needs of the congregation without thinking about what we need.

Identities

We are multifaceted humans. We have different identities that make up our lives—gender, sexual orientation, race, ethnicity, and relationships. Some of these things are more important for some people to claim than others. As we set up our boundaries, it is important to understand which identities are most important to us.

For centuries, churches have taken part in constructing and maintaining rigid, binary gender identities. As a result, religious-based sexism, homophobia, and transphobia abound, and a church might expect its pastors to conform to straight societal norms. If you are an LGBTQ pastor, you might be in a position where you have to rely on your pseudo self in order to stay safe. It can be incredibly difficult to maintain your integrity *and* maintain safety. You may need to stay closeted in some situations in order to be fed and sheltered. If so, you may also need to find ways to protect your core self, such as relying on a trusted group of people with whom you don't have to hide who you are. Some denominations have come a long way to celebrate LGBTQ pastors, but there remains a long way to go. In all of this, it is important for you to make sure your core identities stay intact while orienting your life toward abundance.

When we share an identity with people who have been discriminated against, we continually have to shift our boundaries. Eric, as a black man serving a white congregation, realized this when George Zimmerman was acquitted of manslaughter after shooting unarmed black teenager Trayvon Martin. When Eric woke up that Sunday morning, his sermon seemed stale and weak. So he scrapped his sermon and started writing again about the fear that he had—for himself, but more for his son.

When he got up to preach, he began to cry. As his voice shook, the air in the sanctuary shifted, and people began to fidget in discomfort. He had been in white spaces enough to realize what was happening. He had reminded the congregation that he was black, which reminded them of their black president, and that reminded them of their fading power in the world.

That week, he got pushback for talking about race from the pulpit, and he wasn't ready for it. He knew the dangers of representing all black people in a white congregation. He intentionally worked hard not to shame anyone, but he also felt like his parishioners were projecting all sorts of things onto him. It became clear that the congregation wanted him to leave that part of his identity at the door.

After struggling, Eric realized that he couldn't compartmentalize himself or he would begin to hate the people in the room. He had to learn ways to protect his identity. He had to set up boundaries around himself.

Setting Boundaries

How do we set boundaries around ourselves? When most of us are taught about boundaries, we are addressed as the offenders, the trespassers. We learn how to protect the church and its members. Yet there are times when we need to build some protection around ourselves.

In order to set boundaries, *we first need to understand that we are allowed to have boundaries.* You are a child of God, and you are called to love yourself. This might be difficult if you see yourself as a servant, but the servant metaphor needs to be put to rest. Would you want your child, niece, or nephew to enter into indentured servitude? Why would God want you to be a slave? We have condemned slavery throughout human history, and it's time that we stop using it as a metaphor for pastors. It might be beautiful for the Son of God to call himself a servant and to pick up the towel to wash his friends' feet. It might have been a helpful corrective in the past when white men almost always filled the clergy role to talk about servant leadership. But now we have black pastors who are fighting the legacy of slavery in the United States. We have pastors of color who face constant racism in denominational structures. We have historic gender roles that have looked to women to do the housework and men to run the business. With a more-diverse community of pastors, we have an opportunity to rethink the ways we talk about clergy.

If you are a descendant of enslaved people, or submissive roles have been forced on you in the past, then you may not realize that you need boundaries or that you're even allowed to have them. I (Carol) grew up in a conservative Baptist household and church with strict gender roles, so I carefully watch my white male colleagues to check my behavior. If I did what was natural in terms of my upbringing, I would take up the servant role and be constantly jumping up to serve coffee, making all the meals for the potluck, and taking home the church laundry. I would have no time to do my actual job. I have to set boundaries. Likewise, your time, beliefs, privacy, and identity matter as much as your church members' do.

Once you have established that you can have boundaries, then you need to *identify when you need a boundary*. How do you know when to set up a boundary? Here are some indications:

- You feel exhausted and burned-out.
- You feel resentment and bitterness.
- You avoid certain people.
- You avoid certain situations.
- Your anxiety is increasing.
- You are drinking too much.
- Your blood pressure keeps climbing.
- Your family complains about how you never stop working.
- You find it difficult to leave the office (or to stop working at your home office).
- You don't take time off.
- You feel pressured to talk about private matters that you don't want to discuss.
- Members of the congregation continue to expect that you will do things that are outside of your job description (e.g., taking notes, cooking dinners, or baking Communion bread).

When you sense that feeling of dread or burnout, try to *determine how you feel violated and what you need.* Is it an expectation, a belief, a relationship, or an identity issue? Does it have to do with your time, space, integrity, privacy, or authenticity? Talk about it with a friend, or journal about it until you can identify the issue and state it clearly. You are not trying to change the other person but to focus on what you need. If someone in the church loves to hug people and you're not a hugger, then you need your personal space. The other person will still be a hugger. You have no control over that. But you should have control over who touches you.

When you're able to identify the issue, try to state what you need in the situation. Here are some examples:

- The finance committee chair calls and texts me on my days off. I need an uninterrupted day of rest. (By the way, you can even take two, if you need them.)
- The property committee members drop by unannounced to the parsonage to make repairs. I need privacy and a twenty-four-hour notice for regular maintenance.
- People constantly hug me. I'm not a touchy person, and it feels intrusive. I need boundaries around my personal space.
- I can't save the church. I need to stop putting impossible expectations on myself.
- The Bible study leaders want me to agree with them on every political issue. I need to have my own beliefs.
- My denomination discriminates against LGBTQ clergy. I need to maintain my integrity.
- I'm single, and church members constantly ask about my personal relationships. I don't feel comfortable talking to them about this. I need privacy around my dating life.
- My child is going through a mental health crisis. The church members keep asking me about her. I need to focus on being a good parent without outside interference.
- I am a man who is married to a woman. I'm also bisexual, and my sexual identity is very important to me. Our congregation is not fully affirming. I need to be able to express that I'm queer in my ministry.

The next step is to *clearly communicate what you need.* Different pastors have different needs. You may follow a pastor who loved to go on vacation with members. That former pastor invited members to the parsonage and cooked for them on his day off. He loved to bake bread and wash all of the linens for Communion. You might follow a pastor who loved to do the church's maintenance work, and you could regularly find him on the roof, making repairs. Or the former pastor might have had her entire family involved with the congregation, teaching Sunday school and going on mission trips.

You have different needs from those of the person before you, yet you're working in a system that has been built around the preferences and expectations of former leaders. So you have to be clear about what you need.

Your parishioners may not know that you have Monday or Friday off, so they keep calling. The former pastor may have always laundered the tablecloths, so they don't realize that it's really not your job. An older couple in the church thinks that setting you up with their grandson is a kind gesture, even though you have no interest in dating church members' relatives. Setting up and communicating clear boundaries will be a kind way of helping them understand.

Church members will take as much of your energy, time, and work as they can. This is not because they're evil but because they're human. Plus, they might have also been told all of those myths that pastors perpetuate—that we are the church's servants and we're married to our jobs. They might imagine the Christian vocation as never-ending self-sacrifice to the needs of others. To be clear, there may be times when we need to sacrifice, but we don't really need to sacrifice our day off to hear another complaint about how the Communion bread should be cut into circles instead of squares.

So how can you kindly and clearly explain your boundaries? You can do so by stating them. Here are some examples:

- "I love this congregation so much that I could be tempted to work 24/7! But I know that if I don't take time off, I won't be able to minister well. I'll burn out. That's why I need to have Fridays and Saturdays off."

- "It's great to see you, but I need at least twenty-four hours' notice before I can welcome people into the parsonage. When can you meet at my office? Do you have any time during my office hours?"
- "I'm not a hugger. It's not personal; I just don't like to hug people when I'm at work. How about a handshake?"
- A boundary for yourself: "There are a lot of expectations sitting on my shoulders. I am called to be their pastor, not their savior."
- "We welcome a wide spectrum of beliefs in this church. I never expect you to conform to what I believe. And I hope that you never expect me to conform to what you believe."
- "We have a purple church. My prayer is that we will keep loving and accepting one another's opinions, even when our larger culture becomes more polarized."
- "I know you care about my relationships and that you care about me. I really appreciate that. But I feel uncomfortable talking about my dating life at work. Let's change the subject."
- "It's hard to be a teenager, and it's especially hard to be a pastor's daughter. I need to respect her privacy."
- "I will always give you the respect you deserve, even when we don't agree politically. I hope that you will be able to do the same for me."

Once you state your request, you might want to ask a question that changes the topic quickly. Have a follow-up question in mind.

If you have a difficult time claiming boundaries, you'll need to practice what to say. Practicing will allow you to state your boundary more naturally. It will also smooth out the edges of reactivity and resentment that you might have as you inform your congregation of your needs.

If your church has been functioning in an unhealthy manner and you establish a boundary, the situation might get tense and uncomfortable. You will be stretching your parishioners, and they will want to maintain homeostasis. You might get pushback or even guilt trips. ("But Fred always answered emails on his vacation. He was a great pastor. The pews were full when he was here!") Stay strong, and try not to take it personally. If you can, remind yourself that these church members are not trying to take something away from you; they are just acting from that relentless status quo bias. Most importantly, stay connected with them. Boundaries without connection aren't a relationship, and you can't be a pastor without relationships.

In *A Failure of Nerve*, Edwin Friedman uses the analogy of a body being invaded by cancer cells to define the hostile environment we may encounter in the church.[5] We learn from this analogy that the antagonists we encounter are like the cancer cells that by their very nature ignore boundaries. They are invasive; we may say that their role in the system is to antagonize. We can try to change them (and we have all tried that), but they don't change. We can try to counter them with our best rational arguments, but they rarely hear us. But would we try to change cancer cells? Would we use rational arguments on them? Of course not. We as leaders in the system need to uphold boundaries and, by our example, help others in the system to do the same.

We need to maintain connections, keep our anxiety as low as possible, and remind ourselves that we aren't alone in this. As much as it may feel like the whole congregation is against us, that is our anxiety speaking. We aren't alone, and we need to help the other healthy cells to navigate through the invasion of the malignant cells.

Returning to Sarah

Sarah's affair was not just a violation of the dos and don'ts that we hear about in boundary training. If we believe that she simply needed to be better informed and that another sexual misconduct awareness course would have saved her from making decisions that would lead to the end of her marriage and career, we miss some crucial contributing factors. When we view this as a case of not being aware of the rules or simply having a lack of self-control, we allow ourselves to believe, "This will never happen to me. I keep all the rules." But those rules become very fuzzy as our anxiety level rises. When we recognize that the anxiety level is growing in us (refer to chapter 4), we need to take action to lower the anxiety before it gets to the level where we will regret our actions.

The story of Sarah is not encapsulated by that one fateful night. It took months and years of compounding anxiety until it couldn't be controlled. The story is the burnout and exhaustion that occur with that never-ending stress. Healthy boundaries are not a set of dos and don'ts in the moment. Healthy boundaries are the result of how we care for ourselves on a daily basis.

Reflection Prompts

1. *Identify the issue.* Do you feel anxious or avoidant with certain people at church? Who are they? What situations exacerbate those feelings?

2. *Understand your workload.* Do you feel overworked or even burned-out? Are you doing things outside of your job description that you resent?

3. *Maintain your integrity.* Is there a place where you feel like your integrity is compromised?

4. *Claim your identity.* Do you feel like you have to hide part of your identity that is important to you?

5. *Explore your past.* Do you have a difficult time asking for what you need? Is there something in your past that keeps you from thinking you can ask for things?

6. *Examine your self-talk.* Do you put pressure on yourself? Do you need to set boundaries for yourself around negative thinking or unfair expectations?

7. *Set a boundary.* Can you follow these steps to set a boundary for yourself?

   - Write down how you feel harmed.
   - Determine what you need. Be sure to focus on your boundary rather than on changing the other person.
   - Write down a statement that clearly sets your boundary. If you feel the need to overexplain, then edit your statement. Often a quick sentence can be more helpful. Keep working on it until you feel comfortable with it, or at least until it doesn't feel so scary.

- Practice your statement. Share it with a friend and get their advice. See if you can naturally deliver it without reactivity.
- Work on the tone. You might want to moderate the delivery, depending on where you need the boundary, how dangerous the infraction is, or how many times you've set it. If you feel more comfortable with a joke, that might be a good place to start (as long as the boundary remains clear). If you feel like you're in danger, or you're allying for someone in danger, then your tone needs to be more direct.
- Set your boundary with the person.
- Keep your friend around so you can process any pushback you might receive. If the person does push back, or refuses to keep the boundary you've set, then think about possible consequences.

8. *Process outcomes.* What reactions have you received when you have set boundaries in the past? Can you see a connection between pushback and the need to maintain homeostasis?

Chapter Seven

Forgiving Our Antagonist

Betsy furrows her brow when she receives an email with the subject line "Minutes from Board Meeting." She knows that the
board didn't gather recently, and the secretary already dispersed
the minutes from the last meeting. A pit forms in her stomach as
she opens the attachment. She's wrong. The governing board of the
church met the night before, without her knowledge. As the pastor,
she should moderate all board meetings, and the board members are
not allowed to meet without her. Betsy sits with numb disbelief when
she reads the notes. The only thing on the agenda was a discussion
about whether or not she should be the pastor any longer.

Through the sterile language of the minutes, she reads how the
board secretary received a letter from a wealthy family threatening to
leave the congregation if the board did not fire Betsy immediately. She
sits back in her chair and tries to recall how she offended the family.

She breathes deeply as she thinks about the father, who often dis-
played narcissistic tendencies. He always demanded extra deference
and treated his kids as an extension of himself. She knows that he
opposed her sermons when she talked about people in poverty. He
said that she was being "too political" and objected to her "woke
politics." When he talked with her about it, she smiled, nodded, and
explained that because Jesus talked about poor people so much, she
couldn't really avoid them.

Betsy recalls that the father had been unhappy because the previous pastors had joined the local country club but Betsy had declined his invitation. She had kids in college and couldn't really justify the expense, even at the discounted rate for pastors. Plus, the club had a history of racism that she could not ignore.

The parents asked if their son could be confirmed a year earlier than the other kids, and Betsy said she didn't think it was a good idea. She couldn't see a good reason for him to be confirmed early and thought that it would be best if he stayed on track with the rest of his peers. The parents requested that their daughter play Mary in the Christmas pageant for the fourth year in a row, but Betsy thought that another child should have a chance.

The church members had always acquiesced to the family's whims because the family gave so much money to the church. When Betsy came along, she steered the congregation away from being an arm of the country club and encouraged the members to engage in more social justice causes. The church began to grow, but the old guard complained. They thought her sermons took them on extended guilt trips, and they grumbled that the new people "couldn't support the budget."

Betsy was aware of the problems, but she thought that the board supported her. When she sees the minutes from the board meeting, she realizes that she has less support than she thought. Someone made a motion to ask Betsy to resign. Five people voted against the motion. One abstained. And six people voted for the motion.

She doesn't know what is more insulting—that they had the meeting without telling her, that they voted against her, or that they just happened to let these notes leak into her inbox without giving her any personal warning. Amazed at their conflict avoidance, she wonders if anyone will talk with her face-to-face, or if they plan on dismissing her without any direct communication.

As she feels those knives in her back, she remembers her daughter and son, who are trying to get through college. A deep well of resentment forms in the pit of her stomach. She doesn't know how she'll pay the tuition bills without a job. She becomes furious that a man with so many resources would take away her family's only source of income.

Betsy types, "Does anyone want to talk with me about this?" and sends her message to the group.

When someone finally contacts her, she refuses to quit. She tells the board representative that she wants to look for another position, but since she has done nothing wrong, she will leave on her own timetable. She gives them two options: the board can bring the issue to the congregation for a vote, or they can wait for her to find another job before she resigns. It is a gamble, but she is sure that most of the congregation supports her and will not be swayed by the threats of one member. Plus, the board members are so conflict averse that she's pretty sure they won't want to expose this clash to the larger church.

The board backs down and allows Betsy to find another position before she leaves.

The next Sunday when Betsy climbs into the pulpit, her hands shake. She feels angry and hurt, and wonders if she made the right decision. If she left immediately and negotiated a healthy severance package, then she wouldn't have to face the congregation. She could ride off into the sunset with a stash of money in her pocket. This way, she has to face the backstabbing members week after week.

As Betsy looks at the sea of faces, she notices that many of the board members have not shown up for worship. The two who have attended avoid eye contact. The family who initiated the threat is nowhere to be found. She imagines that she has made a huge mistake, until Betsy sees the new people who began to attend the church after she arrived. They need more than a disappearing act. And Betsy acknowledges that she does not deserve to be run out of town by a bully. She will come out of this ordeal in a better financial and professional position if she leaves on her own terms. Yet she knows that in order to do this, she needs to work through her own anger, resentment, and fears of abandonment. Above all, though, she needs to practice fierce self-care.

As the weeks wear on, it becomes easier to take a deep breath and step into the pulpit. The search process in her denomination is long and arduous, so she has time to face her feelings. She comes to terms with the fact that people she loved stabbed her in the back. She also knows that she needs to forgive them.

She has preached Anne Lamott's words so many times that they have become a mantra in her mind: "Not forgiving someone is like drinking rat poison and waiting for the other person to die."[1] She knows that letting this go unresolved would probably mean that she would experience similar situations in her next congregation. She would be packing all of that baggage up for her new congregation. She would add to her trauma triggers.

But she isn't sure how she is going to let this one go. How can she forgive the board members when they never showed any remorse? How can she let go of her resentment when they never apologized? And what about her sense of justice? Don't they deserve some sort of punishment for treating her so terribly? It didn't seem like they were going to get any sort of retribution, so at the very least, they should have to deal with her resentment.

If you can relate to Betsy's story, then you have survived an ordeal. Being fired from a job in the secular arena simply doesn't feel the same as a church letting you go. This might feel more like a divorce. It might even seem like a betrayal by God. You might feel your whole identity slipping away.

But what happens if we don't forgive? Unfortunately, *not* forgiving tethers us to bitterness and the people who have hurt us.[2] In extreme cases, a person might not just be a wounded pastor but a wound-collecting pastor.[3] Such people never seek closure; instead, they persist in seeing malice in innocent acts, looking for ways to be offended, and becoming ever more sensitive to slights. They make holding on to resentments a way of life and get into the habit of unearthing petty grievances from years ago. In the worst cases they find a scapegoat, indulging in misogyny, racism, or homophobia.

If we know that's not the kind of person we want to become, then we can set our intention to forgive. We begin by understanding what sort of forgiveness makes sense in our situation.

What We Mean When We Say "Forgiveness"

The word *forgiveness* can mean a lot of things, and the shades and nuances change when the word stands in different fields. Forgiveness can be forensic, therapeutic, or theological.[4]

Forensic forgiveness means refusing to press charges or forgiving a debt. Forensic forgiveness might be instantaneous, and it can be one avenue toward healing. For instance, if a pastor plans to pay a lawyer $5,000 to get $725 of back pay from a church, then forensic forgiveness might be a healthier option for him. Sometimes we get so caught up in our need for validation of the harm that has been done to us that we lose sight of our own need to move on and find healing within.

One offering *therapeutic* forgiveness seeks a transformation of the self. In this realm, we long to transform our defensiveness into peace and our resentments into empathy. As we imagine therapeutic forgiveness, we focus on our shared humanity. We learn practices such as understanding the world from the perpetrator's point of view.

Of course, for Christians, forgiveness also has a *theological* meaning. In our theology, we strive for the transformation of therapeutic forgiveness, while understanding that God is in the mix. Our goal is *shalom*—peace and wholeness with God, ourselves, and one another. In our search for healing as wounded pastors, the theological aspect of forgiveness becomes more important because it can feel like God is entangled in the wounding and so God must be part of the healing.

The wound hurts because we talk about our jobs as a calling. Most of us believe that God has brought us to a place to cocreate a beloved community. When the people in that place stab us in the back, that ideal is betrayed, and we might get the sense that God is in on the treachery. We might echo the children of Israel in the desert crying out, "Have you called us to this place to starve?" We might pray, "Have you called us to this place to be abused?" Because our forgiveness might include divine aspects, we will need to factor in those multiple layers as we forgive.

Some theologians argue that theological forgiveness must include forensic forgiveness, letting go of any legal recourse, but we want to wave a big red flag here. We believe that a person can have therapeutic and theological forgiveness without forensic forgiveness. Dangers lurk in forensic forgiveness because religious institutions can use forensic forgiveness to further cruelty. When working with victims of clergy abuse, we often hear stories about denominational leaders compelling the victims not to go to the police or seek justice through judicatory courts. They use spiritual manipulation, telling victims that they *must* forgive. The institution wants the problem to go away, and often victims will go down this path, thinking that it's the right thing to do and that they'll have some peace at the end of it. But that's not always the case. Sometimes deep regret arises because they have worked hard to protect the institution to the detriment of justice and care for themselves.

I (Carol) lived the damage that forcing forensic forgiveness can cause. When I was growing up, my pastor was a pedophile, and he preyed on someone in my family. While my family was instructed not to press charges in the name of forgiveness, it made the situation worse. The predator kept working and moved on to minister to a more vulnerable population. I have always worried that we didn't take part in forgiveness; instead, we let a wolf run wild to attack more sheep.

I (James) also experienced problems with forensic forgiveness. As a district superintendent my role was to inform congregations when their pastor had been removed for misconduct. I attended the Sunday morning worship of a tiny congregation deep in the Adirondacks to break the news of the serious misconduct the pastor had committed. As I was sharing the news, someone interrupted me to say, "He already told us what he did and asked for our forgiveness. We gave it to him, so he's still our pastor." Clearly some steps were missing. Where was the accountability? Where was the justice for the victim? Admitting wrongdoing and asking for forgiveness are steps in the process but not necessarily the whole process.

Your path to forgiveness might include forensic forgiveness. Or it might be necessary for you to press the legal issues, especially if there is a chance that a dangerous church leader could victimize another person. Often, demanding justice does not negate forgiveness but allows you to forgive more freely.

After determining the nature of the forgiveness that we want to strive for, we will want to give ourselves some gifts to care for ourselves.

Gifts

When you became a pastor, you might have given too much of yourself—your weekends, holidays, love, creativity, and attention.

You might have worked straight through your days off. You might have taken too many late-night phone calls from parishioners, stealing hours away from your family to give them to the church. You depleted yourself.

Before this ordeal, you got things in return. The congregation gave you a salary, but they gave you more than that. You might have received deference, trust, and even love. You might have received thoughtful presents, Christmas cards, or thank-you notes.

That might all be gone now, and you're looking at a serious relationship deficit. You realize that your congregation cannot love you in the way that you hoped, and you feel exhausted and depleted. This is a time for radical self-care, but you've neglected yourself for so long that you don't even know what that looks like.

Give Yourself Time

Do you have vacation time? Do you usually save it up for when your family can take it together? You might want to reconsider your plans, because you need some time now. One of the major benefits that many denominational pastors have is study leave and continuing education time. Sometimes we even get sabbaticals. If you've got it, take it. Get away. Go stare at the ocean or hike in the woods for a week. Go alone if you need to. Or take time to be with friends or family (as long as being with family doesn't mean that you're in charge of cooking and cleaning in a different location). You need space. You might object that your kids need for you to be at home or that you can't possibly leave the church. But right now you need your time more than your family or church needs you.

You might be afraid that the church will blow up while you're gone. That might be true, but that's not always a bad thing. The loss of control might feel frustrating, but when the pastor is gone, the bad actors can (and most likely will) reveal themselves. If you as the pastor can manage yourself, then you will be able to manage the situation better.

Now is the moment that you may want to call on your support. Or if you just can't bear to talk with another human soul about what has happened, that's fine too. Vacation alone, or go on a silent retreat. Just take the time that you need.

Not only do you need time away from your job, but you need time to forgive as well. Forgiveness might be instantaneous. You might be over it by Tuesday afternoon. Or you might need decades. You might think that you have forgiven, and then you feel that knot of bitterness hardening in your stomach again. It's all good. God wants you to forgive, but God's time is not your time. One day to God is like a thousand years for us. So forgive at your own pace. You are under no obligation to rush the process.

Give Yourself Permission to Feel

Pastors are not supposed to have feelings. People expect you to stand over a child's coffin and pray with a congregation without shedding one tear. You are supposed to stay utterly stoic in a congregational meeting when a member stands up and says that you don't deserve a 2 percent cost of living increase in the midst of historic inflation. You should never lose your cool, even if a fistfight is about to erupt in the parking lot. And woe to you if you are a person of color or woman who shows anger in public, for even the slightest reaction will be seen as overblown.

Yet you are human. When you are cut, you bleed. When you get hit, you bruise. And when your church hurts you, you feel pain. If you do not feel safe showing your emotions in your context, you may not be. Showing emotion can make you vulnerable in ways that you're not willing to display in front of your church. Vulnerability is a great thing when you have safety to express it, but not everyone has the privilege of safety. Honor your intuition about how and where you can emote.

At the same time, try not to suppress your emotions or numb them with addiction. Find a space where you can safely express them. If we suppress our emotions, then they tend to come out in reactive and unhelpful ways when we least expect them. Rather, find a place where you can name them, honor them, and exhibit them. Yell at trees, scream into a pillow, and cry in the shower. Just get the emotions out.

Sometimes simply acknowledging the emotion helps. If you feel that anger or fear welling up, it's good to ask yourself, "What am I feeling?" You can go on a walk, write in a journal, or even work on a collage to extract that emotion. Sometimes just saying, "I'm feeling really angry," can be a relief.

Do you find yourself denying an emotion? If you tell yourself, *I'm not afraid*, or *I'm not angry*, or *I'm not* [insert another feeling], then stop for a moment and see how it feels to claim the emotion you're avoiding. Try it on. Whisper, *I am afraid*, and list the reasons why you're afraid. See if that actually fits. You may try to avoid what people imagine as "negative" emotions by denying them, but that doesn't necessarily make them go away. Sometimes you need to name the emotion, trace its origin, and feel it. Plus, feeling "negative" emotions (like anger and sadness) can lead to positive emotions.[5] You can't get to the green pastures without walking through the dark valley.

Give Yourself Justice

You might not want to forgive your congregation because you think that they need to pay for what they have done to you. They have committed serious wrongs, and you don't think they should be allowed to continue without facing what happened. After all, if they do it to you without consequence, then they will probably do the same thing to the next pastor.

As we explained earlier, while forensic justice is one type of forgiveness, it may not be healthy or necessary in your case. Your forgiveness does not equal an avoidance of justice. If someone in the church has wronged you, and there is a way that you can make a complaint, then complain. If your situation needs some sort of denominational discipline, then see it through. In fact, it will be easier to forgive when you know that justice has been done.

Ideally, we would seek restorative justice. The two parties sit together, discuss the harm, and create a consensus for what the offender can do to repair the harm. But we know this is not always possible. This assumes that everyone agrees who the offender is and who the victim is. In most church conflicts, all participants believe that they are the victims and have been offended. So the process of restorative justice is not always effective.

If you actively avoid conflict, then try not to use forgiveness as an excuse to avoid justice. You might think that the easiest and best thing would be to leave your position quietly and peacefully, never mentioning how you have been harmed. Unfortunately, you will not be doing your church any favors if you leave and allow the system to return to the way it was. A lot of pastors avoid conflict at all costs, but this might be a time when you need to speak up. It might be more difficult to forgive if you know that your opponents in the conflict never had to face the truth of their behavior.

Give Yourself Forgiveness

You might not be blameless in the situation. You might look back on your ministry and see where you made mistakes and should have been wiser. If you are beating yourself up for every misstep, then grant yourself forgiveness.

Perhaps you have fallen into the trap of thinking that pastors are supposed to be superhuman, that you're not allowed to make any errors. But our fallibility and limitations are real. When you are under emotional, spiritual, and physical pressure, you might act out of fear. Those quick reactions to fight or cut people off can make you do things that you would not normally do. As you think back on the things that you did wrong, give yourself compassion and understanding. When we learn to forgive ourselves, it is easier to extend that grace to members of our congregation.

If you have difficulty forgiving yourself, then place a close friend or loved one in your shoes. Imagine them telling you the story of what they did. Would you urge them to forgive themselves? If so, then extend the same grace to yourself.

Begin the Process

Once you have given yourself those gifts, state your intention to forgive. Each day, renew that intention. Clench and unclench your fists, remembering that one Greek word for forgiveness can be translated as "letting go." Pray for the strength to love.

Go back to the first couple of chapters of this book. Gather your friends and tell your story. You might have been told to "forgive and forget," but it doesn't usually work that way. Deep forgiveness includes a recounting of what happened. The story may pour out from you in different ways. You might call a friend for a gripe session. You might talk to a therapist. You might paint, revealing how your soul feels. You might go for hikes and mutter to the trees. You might confide in a spiritual director. You might play the piano and let all of that frustration pour from your fingertips. You might dance. You might journal. Or you might do all of the above. Honor whatever way the story comes out of you.

You might begin telling the story by identifying the perpetrators as monsters. Many people get caught in this phase of the process. In this moment, a story can become a rumination if you let yourself wallow in the quagmire of bitterness. If you need time there, that's okay. Rumination can be an important part of processing. If you find yourself unwillingly stuck, endlessly repeating in your mind what happened, and you're sick of hearing yourself, then you might want to try the story on from another perspective. Write down the story from another person's vantage point.

As you continue to tell the story, try to recognize why people reacted the way they did. Think about the person who harmed you. If you grew up the same way they did, if you went through the same experiences, is there a chance that you might respond to the crisis the same way? Begin to build a bridge of understanding and common humanity between you and the person who wounded you. Figure out all the ways that you share humanity.

By building this bridge, we are introducing empathy for the person who harmed us. The empathy is not to help us move quickly to some fake forgiveness. It is also not intended to make us sorry for that person so we bypass the forgiveness process. The purpose of adding empathy is to allow us to release our identity as a victim. Empathy allows us to move to a fuller retelling of our own story, one that focuses on who we are instead of what has happened to us.

When will you know that your intention to forgive has become a reality? When your story begins to change to include the perpetrator's story.[6]

Returning to Betsy

Betsy's story might include everything that happened above, but her story of forgiveness might include an additional paragraph that looks a little bit like this:

> "The church board was under a huge amount of financial stress. The board members felt like they only had two choices:
>
> - *I would leave and their church would survive, or*
> - *the member would leave and they would have to close their doors.*
>
> Either way, I would be forced out eventually. Although their decision was painful for me, they thought they were doing the right thing for the church. They also figured that it might be easier for me too, since it would be a quick release rather than a slow draining of the funds."

The story might change, as Betsy's forgiveness keeps extending. The story might include the wife in the family, who has had to live under the perfectionist demands from a narcissistic husband. Then the story might extend to explain the soul wounds of the narcissist. In each revision, the common humanity that underlies each person expands, with greater texture and understanding.

After we have finished that step of learning to tell the story, while keeping the story of the other side in balance, we will figure out how to extract meaning from our story.

Reflection Prompts

1. *Consider who needs forgiveness.* The strange thing about bitterness is that it can spread to accessories. So a pastor might work hard on forgiving the person who is directly attacking her, but then she walks away with boiling resentment toward the personnel committee that didn't stand up for her. Do you have a good grasp on whom you need to forgive? Do you need to forgive yourself? Can you go through this process with yourself?

2. *Consider the three types of forgiveness.* What sort of forgiveness makes sense in your situation? Do you need to seek justice as you forgive? How will your life be transformed if you're able to forgive? Can you locate where God is in your story? Do you feel that God betrayed you? Do you need to forgive God? Or do you need to detangle God from this betrayal?

3. *Think about time.* If you're not ready to forgive, renew your intention for as long as it takes. If you wake up one morning, thinking, "I'm sick of being tied to this person with my resentment; I need to let it go," then you can become aware of the calendar.

4. *Think about your emotions.* Do you have go-to reactions that mismatch your actual emotions? Do you cry when you get angry? Do you yell when you feel sad? It can be confusing to know what you feel when you've been conditioned to respond in ways that mask your real feelings. Were there emotions that you were not allowed to express when you were growing up? Are there emotions that you are not allowed to express now? How did societal expectations form your reactions? Are there feelings that you don't have access to due to your gender or race? Did your father hate to see you cry? If you're a black man, do you have difficulty expressing anger? Are there ways in which you numb your feelings?

5. *Frame your story.* How are you going to tell the story? Can you tell the story from the perpetrator's point of view? Where do you share humanity with the people who have wronged you? Can you list those points of connection?

6. *Seek restoration.* Is there a chance for restorative justice to be done? Even if there's not, can you name what you would want to come out of the process? Is there something that you need in order to move forward with the relationship?

Part Three

Nurturing Our Growth

Chapter Eight

Reclaiming Our Meaning

*In some ways suffering ceases to be suffering at the moment it finds
a meaning.*
                    —Viktor Frankl, *Man's Search for Meaning*

W hy do I have to be such an idiot?" Isabella whispered to herself, intoning her familiar mantra. She beat on her steering
wheel for emphasis. She had just come back from a board meeting,
where she encountered one particular elder who loved to sabotage
her. He had just convinced the board to table an important decision
for five months. That timetable would have made sense, except that
they had already put off the decision for seven months. Isabella knew
that the elder didn't want the motion to go through, so he was using
the guise of collecting more data to put off the decision indefinitely.
Isabella became frustrated that she didn't see the ambush coming
and could not figure out a way around the endless stalling. It made
her feel dumb, trapped, and reactive.

And it brought her right back to those stories that reverberated in
her mind—the ones that her mother told her as a little girl. When
Isabella dropped the eggs that were meant for dinner, or tracked
mud on the white living room carpet, or came in with torn khakis
and scraped knees, her mother would breathe deeply and look to
the heavens. Then she would intone with the poignancy of a perfect

123

martyr, as if Isabella's purpose was to find new ways to torture her, "Why do you have to be such an idiot, Isabella?"

Every time that Isabella faced the elder, she reverted to those childhood moments. Even though everyone else thought that their pastor was smart and savvy, she felt like that child again—the idiot. And as she replayed her mother's cruelty, she slipped into the victim role.

Isabella had found meaning in her life story, but it was an unhealthy message that she extracted. She was always the injured party in her formative drama, and she lived out the same plotline throughout her life. She was the victim, and she saw slights against her in every situation. She got trapped in her role, and that role was leaving her defeated.

As we continue the process toward healing, we need to go back to our stories, reclaim our character in them, rewrite them, and find meaning through them.[1] How do we do it?

In *Man's Search for Meaning*, Viktor Frankl describes his life as a Jewish man in a German prison camp during World War II. Frankl tried to figure out why some men were running into the electric fences and others were not. Why did some men choose to survive?[2] He realized that the men who survived had meaning and purpose, and so he tried to observe where that meaning came from. Frankl's suffering was most extreme, and yet his ability to describe a path to meaning has been followed by many ordinary people, including pastors.

If at this point you feel like finding meaning in your situation would be forcing some sort of toxic positivity into the situation, then you may not be ready. And that's okay. Finding meaning in suffering is a process that cannot be rushed or forced. Take your time. Come back when you are ready.

When you are ready, you can begin the process. One path to meaning includes nurturing your interior, cultivating your love, developing your humor, tending your awe, and gaining your strength.

Nurturing Our Interior

Rachel walked around the Holy Cross Monastery, looking over the Hudson River. She felt like she was melting into the dark woods and rich materials. A silent retreat was taking place around her. As people read and wrote, she felt that beautiful sense of being alone together.

Being alone together is often how social media is described.[3] Yet this felt like the inverse of what happens with digital spaces. When staring at a screen, a person can be alone in a room and meet someone on a tech platform. People think that we're addicted to our phones, but more often we're hooked on the social interaction that happens on those screens. The digital world has been designed for grabbing our attention. Social media algorithms cater to our interests and echo our opinions. They heighten conflict and controversy so that our dopamine elevates us to an emotional high. The internet is the Times Square of concentration; loud fonts, moving pictures, and constant advertisements beckon us into endless excitement.

In contrast, at the monastery Rachel sat in a room with other people who intentionally nurtured their interior lives, and their silent presence helped her to go deeper into her internal thoughts.

She needed the space. Her church had been grinding with constant turmoil because a few leaders with a scarcity mindset had decided to blame each other for budget deficits. She could find a few quiet hours in her home, but the burned-out light bulb, dirty dishes, and endless laundry begged for her attention. In the monastery, she didn't need to cook, clean, or chase after her dog. She could clear her head and move inward.

As pastors, we're trained to nurture a rich interior life. Yet it's still difficult to do, since a constant clatter of noise and entertainment surrounds us. Our email inbox fills to overflowing. News alerts alarm us each time Taylor Swift comes out with a song or Russia decides to invade a sovereign country—and somehow the same intensity follows both items of news. Our phones ping with every text, DM, or chat notification. We have itchy fingers, waiting for someone to like or respond to our posts. All of that can move us outward.

Interior flourishing only happens with intention, while we journal, pray, and walk. It works when we put down our screens and focus. In whatever mode that works, practice is key. And as with so many things, that means we have to make time and space for it. We have to put a date down on the calendar.

One pastor sets aside a monastery day. After serving a congregation tirelessly, she finally got a sabbatical. Her time away helped her realize how burned-out she had become. She didn't want to go back to that state, so she began to add monastery days to her calendar. She made sure that she periodically spent a day nurturing her interior life.

We might feel guilty doing something similar, since we tie work and productivity so closely together in our capitalist system. If we work, we must show something for it at the end of the day—checking off the to-do list, mastering the email inbox, or writing committee reports. Nourishing our spiritual life runs counter to our widget-producing society. Are we actually working if we haven't set up a meeting all day? Do we even fulfill those 40-hour requirements if we haven't compulsively checked our email every fifteen minutes?

Yes. Being a pastor should not just mean writing digital missives, overseeing leaky roofs, and stressing over budget shortfalls. It ought to mean that we tend our spirits and model the wholeness that we preach.

Rachel walks around, trying to decide which chair would be most comfortable, and as she settles into it, she breathes deeply. Sitting with eyes closed and palms up, she opens herself. She imagines her thin place, the place where she wakes up to God embracing her.

There is a particular geography of a soul, and she wonders where God will lead her. Is it the dry and parched land of our ancient text, where the heat invites her to breathe deeper and thirst with longing? Is it the raucous beaches of her youth, where the chaos of whitecaps beckons her to joy? Or is it the Hudson, which flows next to the monastery, where the movement and rocky edges lead her to a deeper flow? She typically needs to be around water. There is something about the moving beauty that recalls the Langston Hughes poem: "My soul grows deep as a river."[4] And she imagines a depth growing inside of her.

The deep river nourishes her. Throughout the year, on hikes along the Hudson, she watches the edging trees turn from green, to orange, to bare, and the water somehow sustains her inner geography. And even as she leaves the monastery and drives along the river, she connects to that flow. Through this process, Rachel nurtures her interior life and takes a step closer to make meaning out of her suffering.

Cultivating Love

As we nurture our interior life, we can also cultivate the love that surrounds us.[5] Byron began to realize the importance of nurturing that affection when three participants in the men's Bible study decided that they didn't like the direction the church was going. They noticed that the attendance and income were lower than they had been in the past, and they decided that they needed to "run the church like a business." They were all businessmen who knew what to do when customers and profits declined—fire the manager. They asked one another why the church hadn't fired Byron. If he couldn't do the job, then they needed to get someone in who could.

So the three men began their attempts to fire Byron. When they realized that it wouldn't be as simple as they had thought (the men had opted out of every board long ago), they began a campaign against him, talking with crossed arms, bobbing heads, and creased brows in the church parking lot to anyone who would listen. They said that they *loved* Byron but that he really needed to go. They needed a stronger leader in charge.

Soon the people who had been trapped in the parking lot conversations went back to Byron to let him know what was happening. Byron couldn't see that these messengers were well-meaning allies who were trying to help him out. He assumed *everyone* was against him. "The church thinks I'm a weak leader. They think I'm solely responsible for the decline in size. Don't they realize that it's been decreasing for thirty years? I've only been their pastor for three." He began to generalize the voices of three particular men, assuming that the whole church believed what they said.

When church members wound us, we can fall into the trap of universalizing the voices of two or three people. We do it because we're pastors, which literally means that we're shepherds. Going after that one sheep is our occupation. We focus on the motivations of the contrarian wanderer rather than those of the content flock. Also, it's human nature for that criticism to ring louder in our ears than the compliments. It sears into our brains. We ignore the twenty-two people who say, "Good job on your sermon!" and home in on the one who says, "You talk about politics too much." In the same way, we remember the bullying from our football coach, the Facebook nastiness from a stranger, and the criticism from our English professor. As important as it can be to focus on the one rather than the ninety-nine, sometimes we have to refocus on the ninety-nine—those who are content and even admiring. How do we do it?

It may not come naturally, especially if you were taught that humility is the most important character trait and rejecting pride means never receiving a compliment. You may have spent your whole life rebuffing every nice thing that people have said to you.

Sit down with a pen and paper, or simply close your eyes and meditate. Begin to think about your loved ones, church members, and allies. This group might include your best friend that you meet for lunch. It might include the hilarious aunt that you could not wait to see during holidays. It might include your brother who died but whose presence you still experience, especially when you talk through your problems with him in your mind. It might include your partner or your adopted daughter. Imagine the people who love you without reservation, and list them. Don't be concerned if your list expands to pets or even trees. You're not alone in that.

Remember the kind things these people have said, the love they've shown, and the support they've given you. When you are in the midst of a severe storm—when you're not sure if you can keep your job and you hear brutal exaggerations of your faults—you will need an armor of affection surrounding you.

Remember Mary, who prepared Jesus for his death? She poured lavish perfume on him, cried tears on his feet, and then wiped his feet with her hair. This outpouring of affection made the other disciples uncomfortable, but Jesus sat through it. He could, somehow, soak up the love. He needed it for the trials that were ahead.

As you reclaim your sense of purpose, you need that outpouring as well. You may not have a dinner party guest weeping with adoration at your feet, but you can think about that great cloud of witnesses who are rooting for you. When a parishioner reports to you how you were picked apart in a parking lot conversation, you can ask, "What would my loved ones say to that? How would they respond?" You can concentrate on the affection that your loved ones have for you.

Here are some things you can do to cultivate love:

- Eat with friends as much as possible.
- Remember the lovely things that a friend said to you. Write them down. If they're in a text or email, you can print them out. Reread them until you have the words memorized. You probably have random criticisms memorized, so it's good to allow the compliments to have more space in your brain.
- If you're going into a scary meeting, wear a piece of clothing or jewelry that a loved one gave you. Then if everyone in the meeting turns on you, you can look down at that piece as a reminder of the person who does love you.
- Listen to music that reminds you of your loved ones.
- Collect rocks, leaves, shells, or wildflowers when you share time with friends. Place them in windowsills or on side tables. Put a rock in your pocket.
- Look at photos. Keep a photo of your beloved community as your screen saver or phone wallpaper. Make photo coffee-table books.
- Let your friends and loved ones know through texts or social media how much you appreciate them.

It is a strange reality: negative comments stick to us. Our thoughts spotlight them, and we tend to focus on them. The loving things that people say to us might roll off of us like raindrops on a waxed car. We have to be intentional about concentrating on them, especially when we're healing from a recent wound. Keep your allies close—in your thoughts, your texts, and (if you're able) your physical space. As you remind yourself that you're a beloved person, you can have some emotional gravity. Then you can work on your levity.

Humor

It's strange to think of a Jewish man in a camp in Nazi Germany working endlessly while also crafting a comedy routine. And yet that's what Viktor Frankl did. Every day he imagined a funny story to tell his friends. It not only helped him survive, but through humor he also developed a sense of meaning.[6]

How do you do that? You can start by laughing—loudly and heartily. Laughter is contagious, and the more you enjoy yourself, the more others will as well.

If you are someone who loves good jokes, by all means tell them. Groan-inducing puns, awful dad jokes, and complicated regional jokes (there are a million of them in Cajun Louisiana, for example) all work. If they don't work, laugh anyway. You can get a lot of mileage out of cackling at your failed jokes, because the actual point is not to be witty or clever. The point is to take risks, be vulnerable, and make a connection.

If you're not someone who tells jokes, then tell true stories. Notice all the absurd contradictions that we live with as pastors. We have a lot of material. We have the church that pines away for young families and then handily rejects every idea that the one young family who attends has to offer. We have energy vampires who suck the life out of any person who shows the slightest willingness to volunteer. We have the treasurer who thinks that the mission of the church is to have a growing mountain of money in the bank. We have churches that will make a visitor an elder the minute she walks in the door, and churches that call the person who has shown up for twenty years "one of our new members." We have the 10 a.m. on Tuesday women's group who can't understand why the women under sixty-five don't attend. We have so many characters and quirks. Imagine telling the story of your ordeal in a way that makes your friends laugh when you meet with them.

Make it a point to study humor. Read books by comedians. Read George Saunders and Amy Sedaris. Watch late-night television. Listen to comedians' podcasts and interviews. Figure out your humor style by noticing when you make people laugh. You may be the dry sidekick who thrives on having a hilarious best friend. You may be the person with cutting sarcastic side remarks. You may have perfected physical comedy and can use your whole body in slapstick. You may be the one who DMs the perfect Zoom commentary, the one who's always responsible for making one of the *Brady Bunch*–like squares burst into laughter. You may use outrageous metaphors, exaggerations, or alliteration. Whatever your humor style is, lean into it.

Chemically, humor does all sorts of things in our brain. Laughter releases endorphins, discharges dopamine, and lowers cortisol. "So in essence," Jennifer Aaker, a professor who teaches humor to business students, explains, "as far as our brains are concerned, laughing is like exercising, meditating, and having sex at the same time."[7]

Not only does humor connect us with other people, but it also allows us to form a certain distance between us and our suffering. After going through a stressful situation at church, Reggie noticed that he had developed an eye twitch that came over him when he got up to preach. Preaching always made him nervous. Now he had to expound on the text in front of people who were hypercritical of him, which sent his anxiety soaring. When he figured out it was happening, he was devastated. He thought that people could notice it and wonder what was wrong with him. With that concern, he doubled his anxiety. He stressed about preaching *and* the eye twitch. It felt like a neon sign that said, "Look at me! I'm scared and vulnerable!"

So he began to tell his friends about his neon sign theory. When he did, he exaggerated the twitch to make his friends laugh. Then his friends would tell him about their own stress. After hearing about diarrhea, vomiting, and sleeplessness, he felt a lot better about his tiny twitch. And, oddly enough when he began to laugh about it, it quit happening as frequently. His humor allowed him to create space between himself and his anxiety symptoms.

Tending Our Awe

Another gift that allows us to heal and find meaning is awe. Awe gives us two important things: a sense of vastness and a need for accommodation.[8] When we allow nature to surprise us, we realize that we are connected to something much larger than ourselves. And then it blows our minds. In other words, it forces us to expand our reality and our understandings.

Amani learned this when she went through a situation with her denomination that caused her to leave the pastorate. She became confused about what to do. She got a grant and started a project working with the children in her neighborhood. She grew gardens on church properties for people who didn't have access to fresh vegetables. As she ripped up pristine lawns, she thought about the burnout and resentment that led her to quit the ministry. She replayed conversations in her mind, imagining what she could have done differently. The bitterness and resentment welled up.

When the children arrived, her mood shifted with their smiles and excitement. They thrilled at how their seedlings had grown. They loved finding worms to put in the compost. They couldn't believe the beautiful flowers in the pollinator garden. Their awe became contagious.

As the season continued, Amani's story began to soften. As she released the tiny plants into the soil, she began to let go of some resentment. Her awe grew along with the plants. She marveled at how each tablespoon of good soil could have more microbiomes than there were people on the planet.[9] She appreciated the miracle of food. She loved how the children could produce vegetables that ended up on tables, nourishing the community.

Like Amani, many people experience a greater awe while healing from traumatic experiences, especially when they delve into nature. As we listened to pastors, the stories of developing a sense of awe while healing were as ubiquitous as the suffering.

One pastor began photographing nature after venturing into the Florida Everglades. He captured the motion and shape of the majestic birds that nested there. We have hung his photographs in our workplace as a reminder of the beauty that we can extract from church wounds.

A priest began to spend more time at the beach, walking along the shoreline every chance that he got. He balanced on rocky jetties. He rarely missed a sunset or a sunrise and often sent pictures of them to friends.

A pastor began to press wildflowers as he healed from his wounds. He went on extended walks and focused on those things that grew up randomly. Noticing the beauty of weeds, he sought out all the nature that we attempt to eradicate and control.

Still another pastor began camping with her family, waking up to majestic pines and coffee brewed by a campfire. She loved hiking through the trails at national parks, exploring the startling beauty with her children.

For each person, nature fed their growth. The awe that it inspired allowed them to refocus their attention on all the ways that the Ground of All Being surrounded them, supported them, and gave them life. Being in nature gave them access to sights, sounds, smells, and textures that awakened them. Their attention shifted, and their ability to notice the miracles unfolding around them made a certain joy well up from their bellies.

Awe is an emotion that allows us to transcend ourselves. When we become wrapped up in the concerns of our daily lives and bogged down by the stress, awe moves us to a place where we begin to pay attention to something bigger and greater. There is a certain comfort in realizing that the budget deficit at church is not the most important thing in the whole world. There is something vast and magnificent when we have a chance to look beyond how our attendance never quite bounced back after the pandemic. Our problems become smaller as our world becomes bigger. When we can begin to regain a sense of perspective, then we can begin to focus on our strength.

Gaining Our Strength

Internal strength also becomes important in our growth. We can learn strength like Mariana did after an elderly man in the church harassed her. She was the associate pastor of a large urban congregation, and the man had been in the congregation for over fifty years. He was the beloved patriarch of the congregation, and people thought that he was adorable.

The patriarch also hugged Mariana invasively, stared at her chest, and commented on her clothes. "You should wear skirts, Mariana! I can't see your legs. I can hardly tell you're a woman in those pants!" When she preached and he shook hands with her after the service, he would boom, "I didn't understand a word you said, but you sure are easy on the eyes!"

Each time it happened, Mariana's face turned red hot. She was so shocked that she didn't know what to say. The fact that he caught her off balance almost made her feel more powerless than the demeaning comments did. Sometimes in her confusion and embarrassment she would giggle. That was the most frustrating thing because the man could interpret her nervous laughter as flirting.

Mariana told her senior pastor about the comments, and he laughed. Shrugging, he said, "He's from a different generation. Younger generations are just more sensitive about these things. I'm afraid that if you're going to work in a church, you're just going to have to learn to ignore it."

Mariana then complained to the personnel committee chair, who scoffed and said, "You can handle this, surely. He's just a harmless old man."

The harassment continued, and so Mariana went to her presbytery's leaders. "You've got to grow a tougher skin!" one of them told her. "You don't want to drag a little old man into ecclesial court."

The church leaders dismissed her at every turn. She realized that they didn't want to deal with the issue. But sexual harassment in the church wasn't something Mariana was willing to just get used to. When she worked as a business manager and an employee mistreated another worker, HR would take care of it. If there was an abusive customer, the manager would talk to that person. If that didn't work, the customer got kicked out.

There were no such protocols for Mariana at the church. There were no rules of behavior. No one was willing to stand up for her, and it seemed expected that she would be mistreated. When she complained, as she had done in other work environments, everyone claimed that the problem was her sensitivity, rather than the bully harassing her. The church was an environment ripe for abuse. Mariana felt powerless and wondered if she should leave the ministry.

Then Mariana found a group of clergywoman friends who gathered regularly for a lectionary discussion. A couple of them had faced the same sort of harassment. They took her story seriously and said, "Oh no. That's got to stop!"

Then they began to work with her on setting up boundaries.

Mariana identified her boundary needs. They laughed a lot as they imagined responses. Sometimes Mariana would joke about what it would be like to just tell the man to "F*#% off!" Then she tried out other, more appropriate, reactions. Since the parishioner often used shock value to surprise her, she practiced her reply to something he might say. She grew more confident in her ability to say the right thing at the moment she needed to.

Mariana's friends practiced poses with her so that she might gain strength and grounding. Since a family member had regularly sexually assaulted Mariana as a child, Mariana had learned to run as a response to fear. As a little girl, she couldn't fight her large, adult predator, so she ran from scary situations. But now that she was older, she needed to learn how to stay rooted and summon her internal warrior. Mariana's friends showed her yoga warrior poses. They taught her to say, "I am strong," as she practiced them. Mariana closed her eyes as she gained more flexibility and balance. She imagined rooting herself in the ground and gaining strength through the ground of all being.

With new balance, power, and retorts, Mariana learned to respond to the harassment. It actually didn't take many words. When the old man began to joke with her, she turned on him with a solemn, strong face, and said, "No." He backed off immediately.

In response to the man's harassment, Mariana found help where she could—and got stronger. It wasn't the sort of "thick skin" that she had been encouraged to develop—which amounted to ignoring the humiliation while letting a man harass her. The strength Mariana developed no longer allowed the whole church to chuckle at his misogyny while calling him "cute." It was an internal strength that gave her wisdom and made her more prepared for the blows.

Mariana didn't have to react many times to the man before he understood that she didn't think he was some adorable, harmless old man. He quickly stopped his leering and comments in the face of her newfound resolve.

When we go through the intentional steps of healing, we often find a strength and resilience that we didn't know we had. We look back on our ministry and know that we can't be crushed so easily anymore. It is not a strength that comes from denial, numbing, or somehow growing thick skin. Instead, it comes from nurturing our support, telling our story, and gaining internal fortitude.

Reframing and Refocusing

Our goal in all of these steps is to reframe and refocus your perspective. Your wounding experiences in the church will very likely shift your perspective to a negative view on ministry and possibly life itself. The suggestions outlined above are ways to try to correct the perspective to a more accurate one.

As a psychotherapist, I (James) commonly experience clients who need to correct their perspective. In therapy we call it the 80/20 rule: 80 percent of what is happening in our lives is positive or good, and only 20 percent is negative or problematic. Yet we spend 80 percent of our mental energy on the negative and 20 percent on the good. The goal is to put these into the correct perspective and understand our lives not from the perspective of weakness but from the perspective of strength.

When we find our strength, we also slip into a new character in our story. We move from being a victim in the narrative to a survivor. And as we begin to understand ourselves differently, we can begin to find meaning.

Returning to Isabella

In order for Isabella to find meaning in her story, she began to journal. She didn't necessarily intend on unearthing her past, but she allowed a stream of consciousness to flow from her. Each time she began to imagine a future for herself or her church, she would hear the words in the back of her mind, "You're such an idiot!" That would wake up her imposter syndrome, which would chime in, "I can't lead these people! Who do I think I am?"

As she moved these voices from the back of her mind to the front, she began to trace those words to their source. She started writing down her memories and reflected on them with a counselor.

As she nurtured her internal life, at first it was almost impossible for her to be alone with her own thoughts. The echoes of emotional abuse reverberated in her mind. Then she learned to have compassion for that little girl. She realized (almost for the first time) that little Isabella was not an idiot; she was precocious and energetic. Isabella had a severely depressed mother who bent to the social norms of her day and gave up her career when she got pregnant. As Isabella dug deeper, she began to understand her mother's regret as she gave up her ambitions. Her mother felt like an idiot, so she projected the moniker onto Isabella.

Isabella had to counteract the emotional abuse, and so she began to focus on the tenderness of her younger brother. They were close in age, so they had always been a shelter for each other. When she was little and got scared, he would tell her stories about an angel with a fiery sword that protected her. When he got angry, she reminded him to breathe. They both constructed a deep spiritual life as children in the midst of the wounds they endured. That connection with God continued.

As they grew older, he became an artist, while Isabella became a pastor. She thought about what he would say to her if he knew that their mother's biting words had become her internal mantra. Isabella knew that the theology was all wrong, but she also couldn't help but think of him as her angel with the fiery sword, not allowing those thoughts in her mind. She constructed a mental montage of all the beautiful things that he and others had said instead.

As Isabella recalled the healing words that her family, friends, and members of her congregation told her, she focused on what resonated with her:

> "You have an extraordinary ability to see the pain of others."
> "When you walk into the room, you have such a calming, healing presence."
> "You are able to see all the good things in people."

She knew where she got her sensitivity. She could feel the pain of other people because she had felt it in herself. She knew that she could walk into just about any crowded room and see the person who was in the midst of suffering. Just as a poker player could see the automatic tics of blustered confidence, she could see the furrowed brow, hunched shoulders, and hollow eyes of soul wounds. That connection of empathy she shared with her brother was something she could also conjure with strangers. One of her friends called her the "soul nurse to the world" because she had that deep understanding.

When she saw the wounds in others, she knew that those persons needed to hear the good that shone through them. She imagined herself as the author of the perfect yearbook message. She could say the right thing because she knew the power of words. She was not an empty flatterer, but she knew from her own longings what people needed to hear.

She grew to have compassion for her mother and forgave her a little bit more each day. And as she did, her story changed. Isabella no longer identified with the jeering names. Instead, they began to roll in her mouth with a curious detachment. She was not "Isabella the Idiot," but she was a competent woman who overcame a great hardship. As her story changed, she no longer identified with the shaking child but with the strength and insight her difficult upbringing produced.

Then, when she met with the board, she had a new identity. She was a different character in her story. She was someone who had been formed with the venom of emotional abuse, and she had survived. In fact, she learned to flourish. Just as the poison in a vaccine makes a person's body stronger, she recognized her internal powers when she endured the abuse. When the elder would sabotage her, she could see his pain, draw from her understanding, and not allow it to fluster her.

Not only did she begin to find a core strength in her emotional life, but when she tried on a new character in the story, her life took on a new meaning. As the scared victim, she limited herself to the victim's role. She was trapped in it. Yet as the resilient survivor, she could show other people the way out. She realized how the emotional abuse had been a gong within her. Certain people could hear, or even feel, the vibrations. They resonated with her, and they journeyed together.

Isabella took on a whole new calling. Instead of a victim, Isabella became a wounded pastor, and with her, others could find healing.

Reflection Prompts

1. *Focus on beauty.* Do you respond to water, mountains, deserts, or the tropics? Is there a natural element that you could connect with closer

to home? For instance, if you love the beach and you live in the Midwest, can you find a lake in your area that you can visit? If you love the forest, can you buy a small tree for your living room? Begin a practice that allows you to notice what's surrounding you. Can you collect flowers, shells, or rocks? Can you take one beautiful photograph a day? You might want to start this as an Advent or Lent practice and let it grow into your ordinary days.

2. *Nurture your inner life.* Can you describe your interior geography? Is there a place you go when you pray? Is there a thin place where you wake up to God's presence?

3. *Cultivate love.* Begin a notebook to write down the kind things that people say to you. Put thank-you notes in it. Treasure them. Don't worry about making it an elaborate scrapbook. Just be sure to keep the small things. Many of us naturally remember the criticisms that people throw at us. Can you value the kind things?

4. *Find humor.* Look for funny stories in your daily experience or from comedians on TV or in books. Can you begin to craft one thing to tell your partner or a friend each day?

5. *Grow stronger.* Is there an exercise (physical, mental, and/or spiritual) that you can practice in order to gain strength? Can you do chair yoga, lift weights, or work with elastic bands? How have you gotten more resilient? Can you write down the ways you have gotten stronger after going through your experiences?

6. *Rewrite your story.* Can you rewrite your story so that you're the hero? Can you note all of the people who have surrounded and supported you? When you read the story, do you notice the meaning bubbling up from it?

Chapter Nine

Renewing or Releasing Our Call

Todd grew up in a family of alcoholics. His mother often erupted in erratic behavior, and his father scurried around, making sure to clean up after her physical and emotional messes. In all of this, Todd soaked up the hard lessons that abused children learn. He had a particular sensitivity to complaints. He could feel the air shift, moods darken, and trouble brewing. Then Todd learned how to calm rough waters quickly and effectively. That skill became invaluable as Todd moved into the pastorate.

Todd served a congregation in a wealthy suburb popular with business leaders and other professionals known for their successes. The members proudly described themselves as type A personalities. They valued status markers such as fine educations, large salaries, and esteemed positions. It was a driven culture, in which people often estimated one another's worth by what they owned, how they performed, and where their kids went to college. Unfortunately, their competitive spirits did not stop at the doors of the church, and they spent a great deal of energy comparing themselves with other churches. They murmured about their attendance, programs, buildings, marketing, and budget. They often grumbled that they were not keeping up with their neighbors.

Todd handled the criticism with grace, trying to reorient the members to building a beloved community, where everyone would be accepted and loved. He reiterated the truth: "We have enough."

The members of the congregation did not respond well to his attempt to shift the focus. They began to compare Todd with the neighboring pastors, telling him that the church was failing and that it was because he wasn't more like the megachurch superstar down the street. "I hear that Community Church has an excellent pastor," people would say. "And boy, is he bringing the young families in! They are flocking to those services. I think it's because of his sermons. I listened to one on Facebook and it was great. It got me all fired up! Yours are a bit long, Todd. Do you ever watch his sermons? You really should. Take notes. You could learn a thing or two from him."

Suddenly the criticism felt much more personal. Soon Todd became the scapegoat for all the church's problems. He was supposed to manage the deferred maintenance, families missing church for Sunday sports, and a lack of volunteers. Todd even became personally responsible for national trends, for entire generations walking away from church.

And Todd swallowed the responsibility. He tried to fix it all. He stopped taking his days off. He cut his vacation short every time an emergency occurred. He left his phone by the bed so he could answer emails in the middle of the night. He scurried around and cleaned everything up, just as he watched his father do in his formative years.

After a few years of this, Todd developed health problems. His doctor noted his high blood pressure. His wife commented on his alcohol intake. Sleep became spotty and rare. One day Todd went to the emergency room because he thought that he was having a heart attack. He found out that it was a panic attack. The doctor gave him a prescription for his anxiety and encouraged Todd to reevaluate his life.

Todd had to move a step back and wonder if the job was taking too much of a toll on his health. He understood his congregation and their need to prove themselves. Their narcissistic tendencies came out of deep soul wounds, and he learned to forgive them even in the midst of all the criticism. But as he talked with his therapist and friends, he understood how the congregation's reactions often triggered him. His rising anxiety indicated that he had become enmeshed with the congregation on an emotional level that had damaged him. With his sensitivity, he wondered if he should be their pastor.

Todd understood that he was not going to find a pastorate or any position that would come without criticism, but he also wanted to be sure that he was not staying in an emotionally toxic relationship either. The question remained: Did he need to stay and renew his commitment to his church, or did he need to release himself from the pastoral relationship?

Ecosystem Inventory

The question of whether to stay or to leave can be incredibly complex. We must pay attention to our emotions, but we can't let them dominate the decision-making process. Our conclusion needs to be well thought out and not reactionary. We might have an overwhelming urge to fight or flee, but we need to take some time to reflect on our situation with a clear understanding that leaving doesn't always solve a problem.

We have so many things to consider. Our lives are an ecosystem. We often have different priorities at different phases of our lives. When we're younger, it might be good to be in a larger community so we can meet people and socialize. If we have school-aged kids, then living in a district where they can have a decent education becomes paramount. A spouse with a hefty income can give you great freedom, or it can bind you to one location for your whole career. We can look at all the ways that our decisions work together. In order to renew or release, we can take an honest inventory of some important questions.

Are you able to care for yourself? First and foremost, you have to think about yourself. Are you harming yourself? Have you taken steps toward ending your life, either quickly or slowly? Do you fantasize about driving into a tree or taking too many pills? How is your health?

If you are actively planning on harming yourself, then please put this book down immediately and call a professional. Do not delay. You are way too precious. If that self-harm has roots in your job, then figure out an exit strategy. There is no calling that is worth your life.

Don't neglect the drawn-out harm you can do to your body. Often pastors engage in a slow and steady self-destruction through different habits—working too much, eating too much, eating too little, drinking too much, or engaging in harmful drug use. If your health is declining far quicker than it would be from the ordinary aging process and you feel too depressed to eat healthily, exercise, or go outdoors, then you need to save yourself. Please, seek counseling.

This book focuses on the congregation as a family system and acknowledges that all pastors have the power to change that system with their participation or rejection of unhealthy habits. Yet there are some churches that are more destructive than others. If you feel like your church is killing you softly, then please leave the relationship.

Are you standing alone? Bad behavior in a church can consume a pastor like a virus. When a sickness enters a body, the body needs a robust immune system to fight it off. If left unattended, a tiny virus can multiply quickly, overtake organs, and riddle a body. When toxic people try to take over a church, the congregation needs a strong line of defense. If someone attacks you and a group of courageous people stand up to the bully, then you know that the health of the system will allow you to get through the ordeal.

However, if someone regularly pounces on you and the congregation works hard to placate the bully in order to maintain homeostasis, then it might be a different story. If you're standing alone and no one is willing to take your side, then you might be better off going someplace else.

Rosa figured out that she was standing alone about three years into her call. She pastored a congregation that ran like a country of medieval fiefdoms. The kitchen, the Bible study room, and the sanctuary all had certain rulers. They bullied any new people who tried to work in their space. They even yelled at Rosa when she didn't return something correctly or if she said that she preferred something in a different location. They expected fealty in all matters regarding the church. The rulers didn't serve on any particular board. Their power went well beyond official church structures—they had real power.

They complained constantly about doing all the work. At first Rosa took them at their word and tried to replace them. But she soon learned that they were not complaining because they wanted to be replaced. They were griping because they wanted to be praised and valued. They became furious with Rosa when she tried to build up new leadership and decided that Rosa needed to go.

Rosa stood up to one of the rulers, on behalf of another member who wanted to host coffee hour. The kitchen ruler backed down. But since there were three bullies (and their spouses), another one would begin to attack her. It became impossible for Rosa to maneuver. When Rosa would try to recruit allies, everyone in the church was so afraid of the bullies that they saw "allyship" simply as helping Rosa make the bullies happy. Finally, the stress got so bad that it began to affect Rosa's health. She couldn't take it any longer.

If you pastor a church like Rosa's, with rampant bullies stomping through the place, and you're the only one who is standing up to their nonsense, you simply cannot hold the line forever. Don't let the stress kill you.

The good news is that you are not their savior, and you don't have to be a martyr. Their health and existence do not rely on you. As one pastor wrote to Carol on his decision to leave, "Jesus died to save the church so that I don't have to."

Is your family hurting? Raising children will be a wild ride, no matter what your profession might be, but if a direct correlation exists between your job and significant harm to your child or spouse, then you must reconsider your job. Do members of the church put pressure on your family to perform or act in certain ways? Is the church affecting your child's ability to come to terms with their sexual orientation or gender identity? Does stress from the job leave you feeling so out of control that you take it out on your family members? Do you find yourself in a position where you have a limited amount of love, time, and energy to give, and you have to figure out whether you should give it to the church or to your family? Does your church put pressure on you to choose the church over your family?

Jessie's daughter had to move while she was in high school. She was having a difficult time adapting to her new school, and when she went to youth group, there was a close group of teens who had been together for their whole lives. They were a strong clique and didn't open up to the new pastor's daughter. Youth group became one more place to feel like the awkward outsider. Meanwhile, Jessie's daughter became part of a club at school where she finally started making friends. The problem was that it met during the same time as youth group. She begged her mom to miss the weekly meetings, and

Jessie relented. The move had been hard enough, and Jessie could not imagine putting one more burden on her daughter.

The youth director became furious that the pastor's daughter was not attending the youth programs, and the fury spread throughout the congregation. Soon Jessie's family became weapons to criticize Jessie. It became clear that the church needed to back off from criticizing her family and her parenting, or she needed to leave.

Sometimes parishioners act like destroying a pastor's family members is just a normal part of doing ministry, but it's not. Your spouse has no obligation to keep the women's groups running. Your children aren't responsible for keeping the youth group populated. And if the church is harming your family in some way, then pay attention. You have been called to the church, and it is not a family arrangement.

Is your family flourishing? On the flip side, don't take your family's happiness for granted. You might have an amenable child who makes friends easily and seems to root and blossom each time you move. But that doesn't mean you can uproot her during her senior year of high school without some long-term damage. A well-adjusted child with good friends and community support may need to stay in that place.

Likewise, if your spouse is climbing the corporate ladder, or just earned tenure, or has a great coworker community, then his flourishing needs to be an important part of the equation. It might feel like success will follow your family, no matter where your job leads them. But that is not always the case. Sometimes success depends on where you are at a particular age or life stage. Finding that magic flow may not be possible anywhere else.

Diane left a position to move across the country. Her husband was in the tech industry and had always been able to find lucrative jobs. He had skills that tech companies sought. But when they moved because of Diane's new job, they realized that his skills could only flourish in certain parts of the country. By the time they figured this out and moved back to a more tech-friendly place, her husband had been out of the industry for too long. He faced ageism and got relegated to retail positions that were far below his skills. Diane realized too late that she should have considered his opportunities and not taken his success for granted.

What is your financial situation? Assess the short-term and long-term financial risks of leaving. Do you need the money? What about the benefits? Could you get a job somewhere else if you needed to? If you leave your job, could you work out a severance package? Do you have allies in the church or the denomination who will support you if you must enter a struggle for termination pay? Could you leave more quickly if you took an interim or temporary pastorate? Would it be better for your career (and long-term financial position) to stick it out and find a position on your own terms? What about your living situation? Would you have to leave a parsonage? Would you have to move yourself or pay for the labor? Buy or rent a house?

Moving always costs money, even if the church supposedly pays for everything. You have to buy trash cans, shower curtains, and shelf liners. Sometimes there is a gap in pay and the whole process eats up an enormous amount of time. However, if you make the minimum salary, then leaving your position might be well worth a temporary hassle.

Sometimes pastors have a "God will provide" attitude about new jobs. They don't really worry about the money as long as they feel called to the place. And while things often work out in the end, they suffer too much during the transitions. They need to pay more attention to the financial situation.

There is a place in between letting golden handcuffs shackle you for your whole life and not caring about money so much that it leaves you destitute. Can you find that place?

Are you called to the church? Think back to why you began at the church. Do you still dream of all the possibilities ahead of you? Are there small coincidences and signs that indicate you are supposed to stay? How do you feel in your gut when you pray about being there? Do you sense God calling you to a different place?

Tim was having a difficult time in his congregation, but every time he would speak about his church, he would say, "I just don't feel released yet." He felt bound by his calling, and it wasn't the time to leave.

Of course, this question can be a tricky one. Even if you feel like you have a strong connection with God, discernment can be difficult. You might feel called to *every place*. Or you might like people, even when they don't treat you particularly well. If you grew up evangelical or Roman Catholic, there might be a tiny part of you that still thinks you should be suffering for Jesus. As baffling as the discernment process can be, it's important to keep praying and asking the question.

Do you have any passion? Do you dread Sunday mornings? After taking time off, do you feel even more drained at the prospect of returning to work? Do you find that you no longer have joy for those things that you used to love, like baptisms, preaching, or liturgy? If you no longer feel passion for these things, do you think you're experiencing burnout or something deeper?

If you think it might be something deeper, can you answer the "why" questions? For instance, if someone asks you, "Why are you a pastor?" or "Why does this ministry exist?" are you able to answer the question in a way that feels true? If not, then you might be facing a lack of passion.

That is not to say that you need to burn with passion and brim with meaning each day you minister. There will be seasons that feel dry as dust. However, if it feels like more than a season and you're beginning to feel like you're stranded in a desert without a drop of water, then you might want to consider if God is calling you elsewhere.

Are you trying to use external changes to solve internal problems? We can get into a pattern of leaving a church when we're depressed or anxious because we think that our problems will be solved when we move to a new call. That honeymoon period makes us feel like we've solved everything! It was the other church's fault. We feel sure that our issues will dissolve, only to find out that the same frustrations seem to follow us.

Randy became angry and frustrated with his associate pastor position after eighteen months. He thought that he was just not cut out for associate work, so he went to another church and became a solo pastor, but the same pattern continued. Ten years and three churches later, he realized that no matter the location, size, pay, prestige, or health of the congregation, Randy could barely stand the church after two years, and he began to circulate his resume at that point. When he arrived at his next position, he found that the same issues arose, and he began the job search again.

Finally, he worked with a personnel chair who would not give up on him. The chair encouraged him to go to a therapist and sort through some of his personal and vocational issues. The exploration did him a world of good, and he realized that he was trying to change his job in order to solve problems that had to do with his family of origin.

If you find the same problems popping up each place that you go and moving does not help, then you might be looking for external solutions for internal problems. Do some internal work. See a counselor and sort out the patterns that you experience. Do they stem from your family of origin? Are you reliving a previous marriage? Is there something that you can resolve?

Are you able to be yourself? Do you have to hide major parts of your personality or identity to stay at your position?

Some external things simply may not be appropriate in any workspace. The church members might expect you to have adequate grooming or to keep a professional dress code. That might be annoying if you're into ripped jeans, holey T-shirts, and a mountain-man shower schedule. But you'll find a written or an unwritten dress code in most places in your life, whether you go out to eat or preach in a pulpit.

Likewise, many employers don't like employees to randomly emote, complain, and curse on social media if the account can be traced to their workplace. We're not talking about those sorts of things.

We are talking about things like your sexual orientation, ethnicity, or creative expression. Is there something that feels essential to who you are that the church is pressuring you to give up?

Mindy's church knew that she was a lesbian, but she could tell that they weren't comfortable with the broader community knowing it. They seemed inclusive, but they didn't exactly celebrate LGBTQ relationships. One elder in particular would say, "I don't care what people do in their bedrooms as long as they don't have to make a big deal about it!"

Mindy was able to navigate all of this until she began dating someone. When it became serious and she began taking her girlfriend to church functions, the unease on a few key members' faces made her realize the truth of her position. She could either stay at her church, or she could have a romantic partner. To stay, she would have to keep denying a central part of her identity and happiness. She had to find another position.

Renewing Your Call

Finding another position is not the only solution, however. You might imagine a possible renewal of the pastoral relationship. But that doesn't mean that you will go back to things as they were before you forgave them. The relationship is different now, and to move forward you will need to take responsibility for your part in the rupture and change your behavior. Then you will need to figure out what you need from the church to reconcile. Write it down and negotiate for it.

Often you will not be able to go through a formal reconciliation process with the church. Usually a couple of people drive the wounding, and others don't understand their part in it. The church leaders may not be able to recognize their complicity, but it is still important that you work for what you need to repair the breach.

For instance, if you're a Korean woman who has found out that the previous pastor (a white male) was paid $7,000 more than you, can you ask the personnel committee to help you? Can the congregation take steps to make up the difference?

There are other ways to get what you need without a formal negotiation process. Think about whether you need to set up some boundaries. If you spend every Saturday working on your sermon, can you find a weekday to concentrate on it, and reclaim a day off? Can you go into the office an hour later so that you can do some yoga or meditation exercises in the morning? Can you take time to process your feelings and emotions? Can you begin to concentrate on working away from the office? Can you find places to retreat and write prayers? Or can you find a great group of friends to meet with over lunch? All of that might go a long way toward helping you avoid burnout and renewing your relationship with your congregation.

If you renew your call, resist going back to homeostasis. You don't want to return to the way things were before you were wounded. If you do, then you'll set yourself up for a cycle of abuse. In order to go forward, imagine what you need to reclaim for a healthy, renewed relationship. If it seems impossible to get what you need from the relationship, then you might need to move on.

New Possibilities

At a recent gathering with friends, a former pastor declared, "I am so happy! I'll never go back!" Nora was talking about how she had transitioned to social work after being a pastor for many years. She had grown up when women pastors were uncommon, and Nora had to fight hard for her "Rev." She endured sexism at seminary. She would hold her aching arm up for half the class as the professor refused to call on her, preferring to hear from the men in the class instead. When she finished seminary she had a difficult time finding a church that would hire a woman as a solo pastor. Every church wanted to make her a Christian education director, a position she never felt called to. But Nora kept applying for jobs because her call felt so important. Eventually she moved to a church in a tiny rural town. The parishioners explained that they had hired her because they "couldn't afford a man."

After a decade, she still encountered sexism. A church in the suburbs with a wonderful music program called her, and this was a step up in pay and programming. Oddly, one woman in the new congregation complained that the search committee hadn't called a man. The complaint spread to other women. Nora was confused. They were all professional women who worked hard to overcome the systemic gender injustice in their own workplace, so she was saddened that they could not see the sexism in their own behavior.

Finally, Nora got tired of fighting. She was done. Being a woman was an important part of her identity, and she could no longer handle every day being a struggle. But how could she let go of something that she had worked so hard to attain?

After talking with a spiritual director, Nora released her call as a pastor. She honored the hard work and decade of struggle. She acknowledged that every life could have more than one calling. When she let go of her need to stand in a pulpit every Sunday morning, something happened. A whole world opened up to her. She began to see many possibilities, as she thought about writing, consulting, counseling, nonprofit work, and chaplaincy. She imagined going back to school. She planned on getting a D.Min., but suddenly an M.S.W. seemed like a good idea instead. Nora started researching social work programs.

Eventually, Nora became a social worker in a hospital setting. As she went to work every day, she was filled with joy. She loved seeing her patients, training students, and working with the administrators. There was still sexism, but the hospital had rules and expected professionalism. She was treated like a person who had actual expertise. There was no wink and elbow nudge at people expressing that they would pay women less or they would rather have hired a man. The human resources department quickly and effectively dealt with disparities. When she encountered a bully, Nora could go to HR for that too. It was no longer a six-year process of waiting for a term limit to expire so that she could move this person out of leadership and pray that he would go away.

For the first time, Nora felt like she was flourishing rather than fighting. When she was able to release her job, she realized that she had a new life of possibilities ahead of her. After a couple of years as a social worker, she believed that she was living into her call more fully than when she had served a church.

One of the important outcomes of healing from the wounds of ministry can be the new vocational possibilities that open. Often we are told, "Only go into the ministry if there is *nothing else* that you can do!" Not only is that a sad state of affairs for the vocation (we only take people who can't do anything else?), it also makes pastors feel like they're called to the pastorate for the rest of their lives. The truth is that ministry can flourish in a variety of settings. Both of us know many clergy who have used their M.Div. degree to pursue other roles. One of the most popular is that of chaplain. Chaplain positions are not as prevalent as they were several decades ago, but there are still many opportunities. From colleges to healthcare settings, a chaplain position offers a way to continue to function as a pastor with many of the same responsibilities but with the added benefit of defined boundaries. Another common vocational option is working as a leader of a nonprofit. Many community programs have values that closely align with those of churches and may even have regular weekday work schedules with the weekends off. Others have found employment in teaching, writing, consulting, marketing, and even political vocations.

Posttraumatic growth researchers note that people who have gone through difficult situations often are receptive to new possibilities.[1] When people are comfortable and can manage their work well, they have little incentive to change. Life goals get relegated to something that they will get to someday. Yet when a traumatic event happens and they have a chance to process it, things that never seemed possible suddenly feel like they're within reach. It's the gift of creative destruction. Sometimes they even feel *more* able to accomplish something when they've gone through some sort of disaster. Suddenly the fear of failure loses its teeth.

How do these new possibilities arise? After going through wounds, we experience a sharpening of priorities and commitments. We begin to understand what is really important in our lives—our loved ones, art, health. We step back and realize that the leaking roof, lagging attendance, and shrinking endowment are not the most important problems in the world.

When church wounds lead us to release church work, we can do the things that we have always dreamed of doing. We can look beyond the pulpit and see that training that we always wanted to undertake but never had the time or incentive to start. We might think about a calling that we buried under the stress of our pastoral vocation. We might not have had the imagination to see new opportunities before, but as we go through the process of creative destruction, we begin to open up to new ways of living out our call.

We may conclude that our wounds are from our specific setting and that we need to simply go to another church. From our past experience or the words of reassurance from colleagues, we might conclude that we have ended up in a toxic church system that we need out of, but that we do not need to get out of being a pastor. In moving to a new church, we need to be very aware of the dynamics that led to our wounding and be proactive to find a church that will not remind us of those wounds.

Researchers also have found that the new possibilities include broadening our emotional capacity. We can have an increased sensitivity to our friends and family members. On a deeper level, we can understand colleagues who have gone through similar situations. Carol began writing after going through a traumatic church experience. Suddenly she had a new sensitivity to the frustrations that pastors endured. She found a way to process her own emotions as well as a way to connect to others. Likewise, James began counseling pastors and working with judicatories.

Returning to Todd

Todd realized that he needed to care for himself, and he started working with his therapist on self-care goals. He began exercising regularly at a local gym and found that his anxiety was much more manageable. He reduced his alcohol consumption, recognizing that this was a coping mechanism to help with the stress and the anxiety. These changes led to much better sleep and an overall better sense of well-being.

Now that he was feeling much better by caring for himself, Todd began to discern his next steps. Although the anxiety was much more manageable and the triggers were almost nonexistent, Todd decided that he still needed a change. As he moved through the discernment process, he came to the conclusion that his priorities didn't match working in a parish. He realized that he couldn't manage his health and well-being while serving in a congregation. As a result, he began to consider other vocational opportunities. While he was considering this, a friend suggested he apply to a nearby community center that was looking for an executive director. As Todd looked at the center's materials, he became excited about the opportunity. Here was a ministry he could be passionate about that did not include the challenges of running a church.

Todd applied, was hired, and is finding this new opportunity a wonderful change of pace. He still connects with many pastors in his new role and feels he is honoring his calling by working on this fulfilling ministry.

Reflection Prompts

1. *Take inventory.* Answer the questions in the chapter on paper. Wait a day or two, then read over your answers. Did you gain any insight by writing the answers? Talk through the answers with a

friend, spiritual director, or mental health professional. What are you feeling?

2. *Take a week to focus on discernment.* Often we flip back and forth in our minds when we try to decide something. It's difficult to sort out our thoughts. Try to spend three days living into one decision. Then spend three days living with the other decision. As you're living through the week, spend some time every day with your journal. Write down what you need, the outcomes, and the possibilities. Pay attention to how your body reacts as you live with a particular decision. How do you feel emotionally? After six days, look back on your reflections. Where are you leaning?

3. *Renew your call.* If you decide to stay, what will you need to go forward in a healthy relationship with your church? Can you speak to people and make amends? Are there new boundaries that you need? Are there things that you can begin to claim, such as time for study or spiritual growth during the week, or two days off? (Clergy are among the lowest paid of educated professionals, so it doesn't make sense for us to have only one day off.)

4. *Build a healthy immune system.* If you don't have a healthy immune system, can you begin to build it? It takes a while, but the following steps will help:

   • Name the problem. We often want to hide difficulties in church and "play nice," but we cannot fight the disease without diagnosing it. This doesn't mean villainizing members or creating an "us versus them" dynamic, but it does mean talking clearly about healthy and unhealthy ways of being in church.
   • Connect with others who see the problem, and encourage them to connect with one another. Sometimes you will need to step out of the line of fire, and that's good.
   • Allow the immune system to work. When people want to set up boundaries in meetings (e.g., an elder explains that he doesn't want the board members to triangulate), it will feel awkward. You might find yourself wanting to smooth things over, make peace, or placate bullies. Try to hold back.

5. *Focus on your identity.* List the things that are important to your identity or to your family's identity. Prioritize them. Are you denying any of those things in order to be acceptable to the church? Is it something that you can live with, or does it feel like you are denying something essential?

6. *What do you need to stay?* Write down the things that you need. Think about time, resources, and boundaries. Do you have a way to get what you need as you move forward?

7. *Could God be calling you to something else?* List all the things you would be if you didn't have to worry about time or money. What did you want to be when you were a child? What would you be in an alternative universe? Keep yourself receptive. Are people around you hinting at new job possibilities?

Chapter Ten

Walking Wounded

As Marcus walks into the meeting of his clergy group, he feels fragile and frustrated. The week before, his church had held a board meeting. At one point in the agenda, the members asked him to step out of the room so they could discuss his salary. They talked about it for an hour while he waited in his office, scrolled through the news, and grew anxious. According to the church's bylaws, the board was not allowed to meet without him, so after an hour he knocked on the door and said that the meeting was out of order unless he came back in. When he took his seat, the board members avoided eye contact and fidgeted in their chairs.

Then one man took a deep breath and said in a tone lower than his normal voice, "After our discussion, we decided that we just can't afford your salary any longer. We're sorry. If we saw any growth in the church, it would be a different story. But we just don't see it, and we can't keep dipping into our endowment year after year. At this rate, that million dollars will be gone in twenty-five years."

Marcus sat stunned. He never dreamed that they would consider cutting his position while sitting on a million-dollar endowment. A crowd of thoughts rushed into his mind all at once. *That endowment balance isn't a static number that decreases every year. People die and leave money to the church all the time. Plus, the stock market is booming. What did they think they were running? A bank? That money was given so that it could be used for ministry. I'm already working at the minimum salary while living in an expensive area. I was sacrificing a lot for them. They're not going to be able to hire someone for less than I'm willing to work!*

The rush of arguments was so furious that he couldn't grab hold and articulate any of them. He just sat frozen. Finally, when he was able to speak, he ended the meeting abruptly and informed the board that they would need a special budget meeting before they could proceed. Marcus needed some time to tackle the crisis.

At the clergy group meeting, the members drink weak coffee, pick at stale donuts, and spend a little bit of time talking about planning for the upcoming liturgical season. After swallowing some coffee to wash down his donut, Marcus confesses that he needs to be honest. Marcus has always presented himself as the pastor who has everything all together, regularly doling out sage advice to younger colleagues. He knows how to furrow his brow and tilt his head with confident concern. Plus, it is unusual for the colleagues to talk about anything more sensitive than abstract apprehensions about their pensions. It is difficult for him to be vulnerable in front of his colleagues, but he feels desperate, and so he explains what's happening. When he finishes his story, he flushes with embarrassment.

But then Marcus looks up and sees four nodding heads. These pastors relate to his experience. Then they open up, connecting his experience to their own. When Marcus asks for advice, they talk about what got them through—strategically and spiritually. They stay beyond their allotted hour.

It is a key moment for the group. They had always gathered together like hard metal pinballs. They rolled in, all smooth and shiny. Then they pinged off of one another as they bragged about their latest programming success. Suddenly, with one of them showing his wounds, they begin to connect with their pain and healing.

Once the insurrection at Marcus's church subsides, he meets with individuals in the clergy group and realizes that he doesn't just have professional colleagues. He has lifelong friends. They are able to see one another with their wounds. They no longer wallow in isolated pain, but they find solidarity in their suffering and meaning in their healing. They also echo the power of the resurrection stories.

After Jesus died, strange things happened. His friends began to see him. Mary found an empty tomb, and Jesus spoke to her as she cried beside it. Then he appeared before other disciples.

When Thomas gathered with his friends, they locked the doors. They were full of fear, telling stories, sorting out their trauma. Thomas didn't believe the reports. He said he'd need to put his finger in Jesus' hands and side in order to believe. Then Jesus appeared behind the locked doors, among his friends, and showed his wounds to them. Thomas believed when he saw where the nails had borne into his hands and the sword had pierced him.

It's curious. If divine power could raise Jesus from the dead, then why not patch up the holes? Why did Jesus walk around with those gaping wounds? The Gospels read as if Thomas could put his finger in the gaps left by the nails in his hands and sword in his side. Why didn't some sort of divine plastic surgery come with the deal when Jesus rose from the dead? What was so important about those wounds remaining?

Peter gives us some insight to the mystery: "By his wounds we have been healed" (1 Pet. 2:24). The wounds somehow source our healing. The resurrected body must have them.

The imagery has echoes of Greek mythology. Herakles poisoned Chiron with an arrow, which left a painful wound that never quite mended. Chiron became a wounded physician. The Persian poet and Sufi mystic Rumi wrote, "Your doctor must have a broken leg to doctor."[1] Carl Jung picked up the concept in his writings and applied it to psychology. Henri Nouwen directed it to ministry in his book *The Wounded Healer*.[2] The ancient pattern reverberates through time and cultures: when people who have been hurt can identify their own wounds, then they can understand the wounds of others. Our pain can extend our compassion and connect us.

As we explore how our experiences in our congregations can activate past traumas, we might recognize the wounds that Jesus wore. Surely the physical injuries were the least of the pains he suffered. The garden kiss, the fireside denial, and the abandoned cross caused suffering far more painful than an oppressive Roman government could inflict. We have a savior who told the stories and didn't hide the trauma.

We can identify our own pain—the aches that come from our childhoods as well as our churches. The constant criticism reminds us of how we could never live up to our father's expectations. Mean-spirited salary negotiations can transport us to our mother's transactional love. The elderly man who constantly flirts with us can activate the memories of hiding from a pedophile uncle.

As we walk around with the wounds, we can gain a deeper understanding of posttraumatic stress as we learn that "our body keeps the score."[3] But we also acknowledge that growth can result from those wounds as well. As we wear our wounds, we can consciously identify our context and recognize our reactions; this can lead us to a deeper understanding of our lives. Then we are able to lead others through the heartache and healing.

Healing Our Wounds

As wounded ministers (we mean that word in the basic sense—people who attend to the needs of others—as well as the vocational one), we become conscious of our own wounds and their origins. In the process, we form deeper bonds with God, nature, and other people. Then when we minister, we continue to make unconscious connections. We have more empathy, knowledge, hope, and perspective as we listen to the stories of others. As ministers, we tend to the needs of others because we have been there.

Our wounds compel us to help. As wounded pastors (*pastor* is the Latin word for "shepherd"), we can lead others through the steps of healing. We have walked through the valley of the shadow of death. We know the way. We have developed tools to facilitate healing in others, and we can help them through it.

What does healing look like? How do we know when we're growing? What follows is the continuation of our personal journeys from the wounds we shared at the beginning of this text.

I (James) have always found it strange that none of my clergy friends or colleagues have asked me why I left. For years, I was asked why I felt called into the ministry. They asked, "Why do you want to be ordained as an elder?" But no one ever asked, "Why are you leaving?" It has always seemed to be understood. Many do ask me *how*

I did it—how I was able to transition out of congregational ministry and make a living.

I left in 2014, and at the time I'm not sure that I could articulate exactly what went into that decision. It was a painful and difficult time of discernment. Now a decade later, I have a better idea of the systemic pressures that led me to leave.

Although it might seem that my experience with my bishop would have strongly encouraged me to abandon ministry, it actually only reinforced my decision to depart the superintendency. I was appointed to a wonderful congregation, and I looked forward to serving the people in it. While I was there, however, I began to reflect on my life and my ministry.

I spent a great deal of time reading and attending trainings on Bowen family systems. The classic model of learning systems theory is to have breakout sessions for case studies of your work in congregations and sessions to reflect and explore your own functioning in your family of origin. As I explored my family of origin, which overflows with substance abuse, depression, and anxiety, I found that appropriate emotional distance helped me to maintain my own health in this system. In my lifetime, I became overly involved in unhealthy ways with my family, and this had a significant impact on my own functioning. In the past, I had resorted to emotional cutoff as a way to preserve myself, but ultimately I found that this was not the best solution and that at times it made things worse. Keeping in contact with my family and understanding the way I would be hooked into the drama allowed me to discover healthier ways of functioning.

I also learned that some of these same problematic patterns had developed in my work as a pastor and superintendent. My drive to "fix" problems often drove me to ignore my own needs and far too often the needs of my family. I thought that when I moved into the administrative role of district superintendent I would have the distance to function better. But while I worked in the position, I learned that there are far more things to "fix" at the judicatory level than there are in the local church. I never could maintain an appropriate emotional distance, and as the demands grew, it was clear that a change was essential.

As I returned to the local church, I hoped things would be different. I was back where I always wanted to be. I had had a deep sense of call since I was sixteen years old. If I could have skipped college and gone straight to seminary, I would have. I was one of the few first-career students at my seminary, which overflowed with second-career students. It didn't help that all through my seminary and ordination process I was given a green light because I had the preferred credentials. I was expected to do great things in the church. I believed this myself and began to drink up the positive feedback that comes when you ignore boundaries and sacrifice self for the good of the church. Whenever I felt the impact on my relationships and wondered if I should establish better boundaries, I always convinced myself that I didn't have a job but a calling. I had to sacrifice more than my friends in business because this was about God and I was a pastor.

I might have been able to navigate the transition back to the local church if my support system had been in place. One of the pieces of wisdom I was given as I began serving as a district superintendent (DS) was that everyone is your friend while you're a DS and nobody is your friend when you leave. I truly believed this would not be the case for me, and yet I found it to be absolutely true. Many of my longtime friends simply avoided me when I returned to the local church. This isolation may have been exacerbated by another support system that was gone—my marriage. My return to the local church happened at the same time as my separation and divorce from my spouse of more than twenty years. I felt alone, and so I coped by doing what I had done so much of my life—I poured myself into my calling.

Although the systemic issues outlined above led to anxiety and poor coping strategies, ultimately my decision to leave was from a calm position. I stayed at that church for three years, and during the last year I worked on a plan for exiting. I spoke with several friends and colleagues outside of ministry to help build a new vocation. Being a therapist would give me the distance I needed and would allow me to still work within the church system, but outside of the difficult position of pastor. As a United Methodist elder I have to have an appointment to remain in the system. Although I could have left by retiring or surrendering my orders, I chose to seek an appointment to extension ministry, allowing me to keep my orders and remain an active clergy member. This enabled me to leave the local church without leaving ministry completely.

I don't regret the decision to leave. It's difficult to watch from a distance as my denomination fractures. The once wide tent is becoming several smaller tents over the same divisive issues that have split other denominations. I watch as the decline I saw when I was active in ministry accelerates. Once-strong churches with endowments close their doors. But I do more than watch. I work with judicatory leaders to help churches in conflict find ways to heal and grow again. I work with clergy as a therapist to help with their personal and church issues, providing support as someone who has known the struggle. And probably most important, I help in my local church to support its ministries and its pastor, Carol.

When I (Carol) returned home from my mid-pandemic trip to Israel, I finally quit crying. But my body held a limp exhaustion, and I felt like I would never revive. It began to affect small things, such as my ability to read. Each time I sat down, I fell asleep. I began listening to more audiobooks so I could move as I consumed information. I could only drive at certain times of the day, for fear of sleeping while driving.

I kept ministering through the heightened anxiety of the pastoral change, political polarization, and the anxious echoes from the pandemic. The church community had been bruised. A good portion of our members either suffered through a sudden death or endured a major medical crisis. The grief festered without the normal support of the community. The unresolved sadness lurked in the congregation. The comforts of church changed. But with all new leadership, everything had to change. We couldn't help it. We were simply different people.

At home, I paced around the kitchen in a daze, texting my friends, "I'm not sure if my body can take this stress." The wounds didn't have a chance to heal. They would respond, "Carol, why are you staying in the pastorate?"

Yet each time I moved into the discernment process, gratitude bubbled up as I remembered the strong church leaders who walked alongside me, the art in the city that nourished me, and the natural beauty that surrounded me. James had an office in the church, and he gave me a perspective that allowed me to stop staring at my own wounds long enough to see how many other pastors were suffering through the same thing. It was easy to forgive people, considering everything that we were all going through. As I looked around, I had everything I needed to endure the crisis, so I became determined to stay. Yet I needed to stay on different terms.

As I noticed how much my body needed restoration, I became more protective of my time off. I made sure that I set aside time to meditate and stretch each morning. I determined to write sermons during office hours (as opposed to writing all day Saturday). I tried to visit a monastery monthly so I could worship with another community.

I became much more intentional about forming friendships. My daughter turned twenty-one, and while we've always been close, I relished her adult company even more when she got away for breaks. I hosted dinner parties. I spent days with Ryan, my friend with whom I traveled to Israel. We wandered around the woods in New York, hiking around lakes and up hills. We watched brilliant sunsets along the beach on Cape Cod and worked on a mission trip in the Dominican Republic. I felt bad for him when I caught myself telling him the same story for the tenth time. So I would thank him, saying, "I could not have made it through this year without you."

And Ryan always replied, "Yes, you could have. But God sent us each other so you wouldn't have to."

The truth resonated. Even though the years were difficult, I became amazed at every resource that sprang up, so that I didn't have to do it alone.

As I write this, I sense some peace on the horizon. Members are beginning to trust me. New people have begun attending. The wounds are still there, yet I'm finding growth, compassion, and meaning through the suffering.

From our personal stories, we can expand on some of the commonalities of posttraumatic growth. First, we cannot wrap these narratives in a nice bow. Identifying, healing, and growing from traumatic experiences is a long and painful process. The messy wounds will forever mark us, but they do not ultimately define us. Yet—this is very important—the benefits of growth are vital and life-giving. As difficult as the journey has been, neither of us wishes we could go back and skip this process. We have grown and flourished, and that has led us to new possibilities in different directions. We know we've grown from these wounds because we still feel led by our call and our spiritual lives have deepened.

The impacts of our wounds are not only professional but also personal. They reveal a great deal about ourselves and how we react within an anxious system. The tools outlined in this book can help us in all aspects of our lives, not just ministry. Lowering the anxiety in all parts of life helps us to feel better about our lives as a whole.

Our calling as pastors is sometimes used as a reason that we must stay in difficult situations and tough it out. Granted, our sense of call does remind us that what we do is not just a job, but that is no excuse for sacrificing ourselves or accepting traumatic injury. Our calling does not root us to a particular congregation, denomination, or role within the church. We need to open ourselves to new possibilities and be flexible about our ministry options if we decide to leave a particular job.

Finally, we never complete the process. There is never a point in which we say we are done. There is no finish line. We always need to gain an understanding of ourselves in order to grow from the pains and wounds of ministry.

Through this process, we build a support system by connecting with friends. We lean on them through difficult challenges. We begin to understand our own stories. As we view the church as a system, we recognize the roles individuals play. We locate ourselves in the system and figure out how we react. By establishing boundaries, we can maintain an emotional distance and have empathy for those antagonists who are simply fulfilling their systemic role. Ultimately this should help us to redefine our part in our story so that we are no longer victims but leaders of an anxious system. From that calm position, assured of our continued call, we can decide whether we should renew our call, find a new ministry setting, or exit parish ministry. We can continue to nurture our growth as we gain strength and resilience. We become aware of new possibilities as we develop a deeper connection with God and those around us. And at the end of it all, we become wounded pastors.

Notes

Chapter 1: Starting Our Journey

1. Matthew 26:6–23; Mark 14:3–9; Luke 7:36–50; John 12:1–8.
2. Throughout this book we use the term *job* because we have found it helpful when a pastor is fired or wounded. We affirm that God calls us to ministry, but sometimes our ministry is larger than the particular position we hold. Using *job* helps us to acknowledge that while our identity or our ministry may shift, God still calls us.
3. "Book of Discipline: ¶ 340. Responsibilities and Duties of Elders and Local Pastors," in *The Book of Discipline of the United Methodist Church—2016*, https://www.umc.org/en/content/book-of-discipline-340-responsibilities-and-duties-of-elders-and-local-pastors.

Chapter 2: Finding Our People

1. Niobe Way, *Deep Secrets: Boys, Friendships, and the Crisis of Connection* (Cambridge, MA: Harvard University Press, 2013), 3–4. Way writes, "In our twenty-first-century American culture, in which vulnerable emotions and same sex intimacy are perceived as girlish and gay, heterosexual boys are described as uninterested in having intimate male friendships, and the stereotype that boys are 'only interested in one thing' is perpetuated."
2. Jonathan Malesic, "How Men Burn Out," *New York Times*, January 4, 2022, https://www.nytimes.com/2022/01/04/opinion/burnout-men-signs.html.
3. Marisa G. Franco, *Platonic: How the Science of Attachment Can Help You Make—and Keep—Friends* (New York: G. P. Putnam's Sons, 2022), 12.
4. Aristotle, "Book VIII: The Kinds of Friendship," in *Nicomachean Ethics*, trans. J. A. K. Thomson (New York: Penguin Books, 2004), 203.

5. Robert D. Putnam, *Bowling Alone: The Collapse and Revival of American Community*, 20th anniversary ed. (New York: Simon and Schuster, 2020).
6. Michael E. Kerr and Murray Bowen, *Family Evaluation: An Approach Based on Bowen Theory* (New York: W. W. Norton, 1988), 271.
7. Franco, *Platonic*. This section is informed not only by Bowen's theories but also by Franco's work. Franco explored attachment theory and friendship, and she saw secure, anxious, and avoidant styles emerge in her research.
8. Jaron Lanier, *Ten Arguments for Deleting Your Social Media Accounts Right Now* (London: Vintage, 2019), 13.
9. Alex Bryson and George MacKerron, "Are You Happy While You Work?," *Economic Journal* 147, no. 599 (February 2017), accessed at https://discovery.ucl.ac.uk/id/eprint/1476830.

Chapter 3: Telling Our Story

1. Genesis 9:20–23.
2. Genesis 19.
3. 2 Samuel 11; Genesis 34; and 2 Samuel 13–14.
4. 1 Corinthians 6:9 and Philemon. James V. Brownson, *Bible, Gender, Sexuality: Reframing the Church's Debate on Same-Sex Relationships* (Grand Rapids, MI: W. B. Eerdmans, 2013), 42–43. Brownson explains that *arsenkoites* and *malakos* in 1 Corinthians 6:9 refer to the Greek practice of pederasty.
5. Michael E. Kerr and Murray Bowen, *Family Evaluation: An Approach Based on Bowen Theory* (New York: W. W. Norton, 1988), 89.
6. Bessel A. Van der Kolk, *The Body Keeps the Score: Brain, Mind, and Body in the Healing of Trauma* (New York: Penguin, 2015), 21. Throughout the book, Van der Kolk explores the relationship between trauma, stories, and creating a sense of safety.
7. J. Dana Trent, *One Breath at a Time: A Skeptic's Guide to Christian Meditation* (Nashville: Upper Room, 2019), 52–54.
8. Omar Reda, *The Wounded Healer: The Pain and Joy of Caregiving* (New York: W. W. Norton, 2022), 40. Reda explains, "An unacknowledged trauma story leaves its imprints on our DNA and on the way it is read and transcribed, which risks perpetrating the impacts of trauma transgenerationally."
9. Homeostasis is the systems way to keep the status quo. We will discuss this in greater detail in the next chapter.
10. Arthur Paul Boers, *Never Call Them Jerks: Healthy Responses to Difficult Behavior* (New York: Rowman & Littlefield, 1999).
11. Richard G. Tedeschi and L. G. Calhoun, "Posttraumatic Growth: Conceptual Foundations and Empirical Evidence," *Psychological Inquiry* 15, no. 1 (January 2004): 1–18.
12. Marisa G. Franco, *Platonic: How the Science of Attachment Can Help You Make—and Keep—Friends* (New York: G. P. Putnam's Sons, 2022), 93–134.

Chapter 4: Identifying Our Context

1. Ryan Nobles, "Marjorie Taylor Greene Compares House Mask Mandates to the Holocaust," CNN, May 22, 2021, https://www.cnn.com/2021/05/21/politics/marjorie-taylor-greene-mask-mandates-holocaust/index.html.
2. Virginia Satir, *The New Peoplemaking* (Palo Alto, CA: Science and Behavior Books, 1988), 137–38.
3. "Book of Discipline: ¶ 304: Qualifications for Ordination," in *The Book of Discipline of the United Methodist Church—2016*, https://www.umc.org/en/content/book-of-discipline-304-qualifications-for-ordination.
4. Edwin Friedman, *Generation to Generation: Family Process in Church and Synagogue* (New York: Guilford Press, 1985), 23. There are so many good things in Rabbi Friedman's work, although his persistent defense of colonialism can be frustrating. As we lift up the core of his work and recognize all that he has done for congregations, we also condemn his celebration of occupation and exploitation.
5. As Viktor Frankl states, "I consider it a dangerous misconception of mental hygiene to assume that what man needs in the first place is equilibrium or, as it is called in biology, 'homeostasis' . . . What man actually needs is not a tensionless state but rather the striving and struggling for a worthwhile goal." Viktor E. Frankl, *Man's Search for Meaning* (Boston: Beacon Press, 2006), 65.
6. Michael E. Kerr and Murray Bowen, *Family Evaluation: An Approach Based on Bowen Theory* (New York: W. W. Norton, 1988), 221.
7. Ronald A. Heifetz, *Leadership without Easy Answers* (Cambridge, MA: Belknap Press of Harvard University Press, 2003), 73.
8. Edwin H. Friedman, *A Failure of Nerve: Leadership in the Age of the Quick Fix* (New York: Church Publishing, 2017), 246.

Chapter 5: Recognizing Our Reactions

1. Edwin Friedman used the term "non-anxious presence." We don't believe that ridding ourselves of all anxiety is possible, but we can strive for a less anxious presence.
2. Michael E. Kerr and Murray Bowen, *Family Evaluation: An Approach Based on Bowen Theory* (New York: W. W. Norton, 1988), 134.
3. This is tricky, especially when it comes to gender and race. For instance, Emily Nagoski and Amelia Nagoski write about women who have "human giver syndrome." One way that you know you're a human giver (as opposed to a human being) is if you believe you have a moral obligation to be "pretty, happy, calm, generous, and attentive to others." Patriarchal constructs in our society demand that women and people of color ignore or suppress their fear or anger in order to stay "calm" in the face of abuse. We are not advocating this. Instead, we're hoping that we can learn to express and process our emotions in ways that lead us to lower our anxiety. Emily Nagoski and Amelia Nagoski, *Burnout: The Secret to Unlocking the Stress Cycle* (London: Vermilion, 2020), 62–63.

4. J. Dana Trent, *One Breath at a Time: A Skeptic's Guide to Christian Meditation* (Nashville: Upper Room, 2019), 52–54.

5. Bessel Van der Kolk, *The Body Keeps the Score: Brain, Mind, and Body in the Healing of Trauma* (New York: Penguin, 2015), 38.

6. Omar Reda, *The Wounded Healer: The Pain and Joy of Caregiving* (New York: W. W. Norton, 2022), 33.

7. I (Carol) resisted yoga for many years because of the cultural-appropriation aspects of it, but I gave in when my doctor recommended it. It has been invaluable as I've healed from trauma. To read more, see Van der Kolk, *Body Keeps the Score*, 86.

8. Amanda Ripley, *High Conflict: Why We Get Trapped and How We Get Out* (New York: Simon & Schuster, 2022), 91–101.

Chapter 6: Setting Our Boundaries

1. Michael E. Kerr and Murray Bowen, *Family Evaluation: An Approach Based on Bowen Theory* (New York: W. W. Norton, 1988), 176.

2. Edwin H. Friedman, *A Failure of Nerve: Leadership in the Age of the Quick Fix* (New York: Church Publishing, 2017), 67.

3. Kevin Quealy, "Your Rabbi? Probably a Democrat. Your Baptist Pastor? Probably a Republican. Your Priest? Who Knows," *New York Times*, June 12, 2017, https://www.nytimes.com/interactive/2017/06/12/upshot/the-politics-of-americas-religious-leaders.html.

4. The author Brian McLaren often claims that Fox News has become the most influential religion for many Christians in the United States.

5. Friedman, *Failure of Nerve*, 138–42.

Chapter 7: Forgiving Our Antagonist

1. Anne Lamott, *Traveling Mercies: Some Thoughts on Faith* (New York: Anchor Books, 2006), 134.

2. Desmond Tutu and Mpho Tutu, *The Book of Forgiving: The Fourfold Path for Healing Ourselves and Our World* (San Francisco: HarperOne, 2015), 16.

3. "Wound collectors" intentionally look for and collect social slights for their personal benefit in a way that's toxic or pathological. Joe Navarro, "Wound Collectors," *Psychology Today*, April 7, 2013, https://www.psychologytoday.com/us/blog/spycatcher/201304/wound-collectors.

4. Here we are relying on the important work of F. LeRon Shults and Steven J. Sandage, *The Faces of Forgiveness: Searching for Wholeness and Salvation* (Grand Rapids: Baker Academic, 2003), 20–26, as our touchstone, although our definitions ultimately stray from their understandings.

5. Tori Rodriguez, "Negative Emotions Are Key to Well-Being," *Scientific American*, May 1, 2013, https://www.scientificamerican.com/article/negative-emotions-key-well-being.

6. Tutu and Tutu, *Book of Forgiving*, 133.

Chapter 8: Reclaiming Our Meaning

1. Viktor E. Frankl, *Man's Search for Meaning* (Boston: Beacon Press, 2006).
2. Frankl, *Man's Search for Meaning*, 18.
3. Sherry Turkle, *Alone Together: Why We Expect More from Technology and Less from Each Other* (New York: Basic Books, 2017).
4. Langston Hughes, "The Negro Speaks of Rivers," Poetry Foundation, https://www.poetryfoundation.org/poems/44428/the-negro-speaks-of-rivers.
5. Frankl, *Man's Search for Meaning*, 37.
6. Frankl, *Man's Search for Meaning*, 43–44.
7. Jennifer Aaker and Naomi Bagdonas, "Why Great Leaders Take Humor Seriously," TED Talk, https://www.ted.com/talks/jennifer_aaker_and_naomi_bagdonas_why_great_leaders_take_humor_seriously?language=en. Aaker and Bagdonas are the authors of *Humor, Seriously: Why Humor Is a Secret Weapon in Business and Life (And How Anyone Can Harness It. Even You.)* (New York: Currency, 2021).
8. Anna Mikulak, "All about Awe," Association for Psychological Science, March 31, 2015, https://www.psychologicalscience.org/observer/all-about-awe.
9. Mary Beth Albright, *Eat and Flourish: How Food Supports Emotional Well-Being* (New York: Countryman Press, 2023), 40.

Chapter 9: Renewing or Releasing Our Call

1. Richard G. Tedeschi and L. G. Calhoun. "Posttraumatic Growth: Conceptual Foundations and Empirical Evidence," *Psychological Inquiry* 15, no. 1 (January 2004): 1–18.

Chapter 10: Walking Wounded

1. Coleman Barks and Jalāl al-Dīn Rūmī, "Childhood Friends (3)," in *A Year with Rumi: Daily Readings* (San Francisco: HarperOne, 2006), 306.
2. Henri J. M. Nouwen, *The Wounded Healer: Ministry in Contemporary Society* (New York: Image Books, 2010).
3. Bessel Van der Kolk, *The Body Keeps the Score: Brain, Mind, and Body in the Healing of Trauma* (New York: Penguin, 2015).

Bibliography

Aristotle. "Book VIII: The Kinds of Friendship." In *Nicomachean Ethics*. Translated by J. A. K. Thomson. London: Penguin Group, 2004.

Bowen, Murray. *Family Therapy in Clinical Practice*. Lanham, MD: Rowman & Littlefield, 2004.

Brownson, James V. *Bible, Gender, Sexuality: Reframing the Church's Debate on Same-Sex Relationships*. Grand Rapids, MI: W. B. Eerdmans, 2013.

Creech, R. Robert. *Family Systems and Congregational Life: A Map for Ministry*. Grand Rapids, MI: Baker Academic, 2019.

Franco, Marisa G. *Platonic: How the Science of Attachment Can Help You Make—and Keep—Friends*. New York: G. P. Putnam's Sons, 2022.

Frankl, Viktor E. *Man's Search for Meaning*. Boston: Beacon Press, 2006.

Friedman, Edwin H. *A Failure of Nerve: Leadership in the Age of the Quick Fix*. New York: Church Publishing, 2017.

Friedman, Edwin H. *Friedman's Fables*. New York: Guilford Press, 2014.

Friedman, Edwin H. *Generation to Generation: Family Process in Church and Synagogue*. New York: Guilford Press, 2011.

Heifetz, Ronald A. *Leadership without Easy Answers*. Cambridge, MA: Belknap Press of Harvard University Press, 2003.

Kerr, Michael E. *Bowen Theory's Secrets: Revealing the Hidden Life of Families*. New York: W. W. Norton, 2022.

Kerr, Michael E., and Murray Bowen. *Family Evaluation: An Approach Based on Bowen Theory*. New York: W. W. Norton, 1988.

Kerr, Michael E., and Ruth Riley Sagar. *One Family's Story: A Primer on Bowen Theory*. Washington, DC: Bowen Center for the Study of the Family, Georgetown Family Center, 2013.

Lamott, Anne. *Traveling Mercies: Some Thoughts on Faith*. New York: Anchor Books, 2006.

Lanier, Jaron. *Ten Arguments for Deleting Your Social Media Accounts Right Now*. London: Vintage, 2019.

Nagoski, Emily, and Amelia Nagoski. *Burnout: The Secret to Unlocking the Stress Cycle*. London: Vermilion, 2020.

Navarro, Joe. "Wound Collectors." *Psychology Today*. April 7, 2013. https://www.psychologytoday.com/us/blog/spycatcher/201304/wound-collectors.

Noone, Robert J. *Family and Self: Bowen Theory and the Shaping of Adaptive Capacity*. Lanham, MD: Lexington Books, 2021.

Noone, Robert J., and Daniel V. Papero. *The Family Emotional System: An Integrative Concept for Theory, Science, and Practice*. Lanham, MD: Lexington Books, 2017.

Putnam, Robert D. *Bowling Alone: The Collapse and Revival of American Community*. 20th anniversary ed. New York: Simon & Schuster, 2020.

Reda, Omar. *The Wounded Healer: The Pain and Joy of Caregiving*. New York: W. W. Norton, 2022.

Ripley, Amanda. *High Conflict: Why We Get Trapped and How We Get Out*. New York: Simon & Schuster, 2022.

Rodriguez, Tori. "Negative Emotions Are Key to Well-Being." *Scientific American*. May 1, 2013. https://www.scientificamerican.com/article/negative-emotions-key-well-being.

Shults, F. LeRon, and Steven J. Sandage. *The Faces of Forgiveness: Searching for Wholeness and Salvation*. Grand Rapids, MI: Baker Academic, 2003.

Steinke, Peter L. *Congregational Leadership in Anxious Times: Being Calm and Courageous No Matter What*. Herndon, VA: Alban Institute, 2014.

Steinke, Peter L. *How Your Church Family Works: Understanding Congregations as Emotional Systems*. Herndon, VA: Alban Institute, 2006.

Steinke, Peter L. *Uproar: Calm Leadership in Anxious Times*. Lanham, MD: Rowman & Littlefield, 2019.

Tedeschi, R. G., and L. G. Calhoun. "Posttraumatic Growth: Conceptual Foundations and Empirical Evidence." *Psychological Inquiry* 15, no. 1 (January 2004): 1–18.

Titelman, Peter. *Differentiation of Self: Bowen Family Systems Theory Perspectives*. New York: Routledge, 2015.

Trent, J. Dana. *One Breath at a Time: A Skeptic's Guide to Christian Meditation*. Nashville: Upper Room, 2019.

Tutu, Desmond, and Mpho Tutu. *The Book of Forgiving: The Fourfold Path for Healing Ourselves and Our World*. San Francisco: HarperOne, 2015.

Van der Kolk, Bessel. *The Body Keeps the Score: Brain, Mind, and Body in the Healing of Trauma*. New York: Penguin, 2015.

Way, Niobe. *Deep Secrets: Boys, Friendships, and the Crisis of Connection*. Cambridge, MA: Harvard University Press, 2013.

* 9 7 8 0 6 6 4 2 6 8 4 5 9 *